TYPE 2 DIABETES COOKBOOK FOR BEGINNERS

1200 Days of Easy & Tasty Diabetic Recipes with a 30 Days Meal Plan to Lower Your Blood Sugar and Help you Achieve a Better Lifestyle

Poula Ray

© Copyright 2022 by Poula Ray - All rights reserved.

This document is geared towards providing exact and reliable information in regards to the topic and issue covered. The publication is sold with the idea that the publisher is not required to render accounting, officially permitted, or otherwise, qualified services. If advice is necessary, legal or professional, a practiced individual in the profession should be ordered.

- From a Declaration of Principles which was accepted and approved equally by a Committee of the American Bar Association and a Committee of Publishers and Associations.

In no way is it legal to reproduce, duplicate, or transmit any part of this document in either electronic means or in printed format. Recording of this publication is strictly prohibited and any storage of this document is not allowed unless with written permission from the publisher. All rights reserved.

The information provided herein is stated to be truthful and consistent, in that any liability, in terms of inattention or otherwise, by any usage or abuse of any policies, processes, or Instructions: contained within is the solitary and utter responsibility of the recipient reader. Under no circumstances will any legal responsibility or blame be held against the publisher for any reparation, damages, or monetary loss due to the information herein, either directly or indirectly.

Respective authors own all copyrights not held by the publisher.

The information herein is offered for informational purposes solely, and is universal as so. The presentation of the information is without contract or any type of guarantee assurance.

The trademarks that are used are without any consent, and the publication of the trademark is without permission or backing by the trademark owner. All trademarks and brands within this book are for clarifying purposes only and are the owned by the owners themselves, not affiliated with this document.

Table of Contents

1. **INTRODUCTION** 7
1. Tips for Living a Better Journey on a Diabetic Lifestyle 7

CHAPTER 1: BREAKFAST RECIPES 10

- RECIPE 1: Almond Quinoa with Cranberries 10
- RECIPE 2: Apple Spiced Overnight Oats 11
- RECIPE 3: Avocado and Goat Cheese Toast 12
- RECIPE 4: Bagel with Poached Egg 13
- RECIPE 5: Baked Eggs 14
- RECIPE 6: Banana Bread French Toast 15
- RECIPE 7: Black Bean and Egg Tacos 16
- RECIPE 8: Brussels Sprout with Fried Eggs 17
- RECIPE 9: Bulgur Porridge 18
- RECIPE 10: Cauliflower Cups 19
- RECIPE 11: Cauliflower Fritters 20
- RECIPE 12: Chicken Nacho Casserole 21
- RECIPE 13: Egg and Ham Burrito 22
- RECIPE 14: Egg and Spinach Breakfast Burritos 23
- RECIPE 15: Feta Scrambled Egg Wraps 24
- RECIPE 16: Honey French Toast 25
- RECIPE 17: Mushroom Breakfast Burrito 26
- RECIPE 18: Omelet with Turmeric 27
- RECIPE 19: Parmesan Herb Frittata 28
- RECIPE 20: Parsley Chicken Breast 29
- RECIPE 21: Potato-Bacon Gratin 30
- RECIPE 22: Pumpkin Pancakes 31
- RECIPE 23: Quinoa Burrito 32
- RECIPE 24: Sausage Tortilla Breakfast Bake 33
- RECIPE 25: Savory Egg Muffins 34
- RECIPE 26: Scrambled Yellow Tofu 35
- RECIPE 27: Spicy Jalapeno Popper Deviled Eggs 36
- RECIPE 28: Sweet Potato Hash 37
- RECIPE 29: Walnut and Oat Granola 38
- RECIPE 30: Zucchini and Yellow Pepper Scramble 39

CHAPTER 2: LUNCH RECIPES — 40

- RECIPE 31: Baked Penne Pasta 40
- RECIPE 32: Beef and Mushroom Casserole 42
- RECIPE 33: Butter Beef and Spinach 43
- RECIPE 34: Buttery Lemon Chicken 44
- RECIPE 35: Buttery Pot Roast 45
- RECIPE 36: Cabbage and Meat Gravy 46
- RECIPE 37: Cheesy Beef and Broccoli 47
- RECIPE 38: Chicken Casablanca 48
- RECIPE 39: Chicken Ricotta 49
- RECIPE 40: Crispy Dill Salmon 50
- RECIPE 41: Feta and Sun-Dried Tomatoes Prawns 51
- RECIPE 42: Garlic Galore Rotisserie Chicken 52
- RECIPE 43: Garlic Honey Chicken 53
- RECIPE 44: Hawaiian Chicken Packets 54
- RECIPE 45: Lamb and Pine Nut Aubergine 55
- RECIPE 46: Lamb Shanks with Burgundy Sauce 56
- RECIPE 47: Lemon Pepper Tilapia with Broccoli and Carrots ... 57
- RECIPE 48: Lime Lamb Chops 58
- RECIPE 49: Lime Pulled Pork 59
- RECIPE 50: Maple Pork with Figs 60
- RECIPE 51: Pistachios and Herb Halibut 61
- RECIPE 52: Pork Chops with Apple Stuffing 62
- RECIPE 53: Roast Chicken Casserole 63
- RECIPE 54: Roast Pork Tenderloin with Apple Slaw 64
- RECIPE 55: Salisbury Steak in Mushroom Sauce 65
- RECIPE 56: Sausage Pasta 66
- RECIPE 57: Sesame Chicken with Couscous 67
- RECIPE 58: Sweet and Tangy Salmon 68
- RECIPE 59: Thyme Turkey Breast 69
- RECIPE 60: Walnut and Oat-Crusted Cod 70

CHAPTER 3: DINNER RECIPES — 71

- RECIPE 61: Artichoke Ratatouille Chicken 71
- RECIPE 62: Baked Turkey Spaghetti 72
- RECIPE 63: Basil Grilled Shrimp 73

RECIPE 64:	CAJUN COCONUT CREAM PRAWNS	74
RECIPE 65:	CHICKEN AND APRICOT TAGINE	75
RECIPE 66:	CHICKEN FAJITAS	76
RECIPE 67:	CHICKEN WITH BELL PEPPER THYME SAUCE	77
RECIPE 68:	CHILI PORK TENDERLOIN	78
RECIPE 69:	CINNAMON CHICKEN	79
RECIPE 70:	CRUSTED RED SNAPPER	80
RECIPE 71:	CURRY TURKEY STIR-FRY	81
RECIPE 72:	GINGER COD CHARD BAKE	82
RECIPE 73:	HALIBUT CEVICHE WITH CILANTRO	83
RECIPE 74:	HERB-GRILLED BASS	84
RECIPE 75:	LIME AND ORANGE GRILLED SCALLOPS	85
RECIPE 76:	MUSSELS IN TOMATO SAUCE	86
RECIPE 77:	ORANGE TILAPIA	87
RECIPE 78:	PEPPERY HALIBUT FILLET WITH BEANS	88
RECIPE 79:	RICOTTA AND TURKEY BELL PEPPERS	89
RECIPE 80:	ROASTED BEEF WITH SHALLOT SAUCE	90
RECIPE 81:	ROASTED SEA BASS	91
RECIPE 82:	ROASTED TILAPIA AND TOMATOES WITH GARLIC	92
RECIPE 83:	ROSEMARY CHICKEN	93
RECIPE 84:	SALMON FISH CAKES	94
RECIPE 85:	SALMON IN GINGER CREAM	95
RECIPE 86:	SESAME TURKEY STIR-FRY	96
RECIPE 87:	SHRIMP WITH FRESH PARSLEY	97
RECIPE 88:	TENDER TURKEY WITH HERBS	98
RECIPE 89:	TURKEY PATTIES WITH DARK ONION GRAVY	99
RECIPE 90:	ZUCCHINI CARBONARA	100

CHAPTER 4:	**DESSERT RECIPES**	**101**
RECIPE 91:	BAKED MAPLE CUSTARD	101
RECIPE 92:	BLUEBERRY CRISP	102
RECIPE 93:	BLUEBERRY MUFFINS	103
RECIPE 94:	CARROT CUPCAKES	104
RECIPE 95:	CHOCOLATE ORANGE BREAD PUDDING	105
RECIPE 96:	FIG AND WALNUT YOGURT TARTS	106
RECIPE 97:	FROZEN LEMON AND BLUEBERRY	107

Recipe 98:	Lemon Chiffon with Fresh Berries	108
Recipe 99:	Nut Squares	109
Recipe 100:	Peanut Butter Cups	110

11.   CONCLUSION   111

12.   INDEX   113

1. Introduction

Diabetes is actually a chronic condition that impairs your body's ability to turn food into energy. If you actually have diabetes, your body either doesn't utilize insulin properly or doesn't produce enough insulin. Although there is currently no actual cure for diabetes, losing weight, eating healthy meals, and being active may help. Taking your medicine as directed, getting diabetes self-management education and support, and going to your doctor's appointments may help you manage your diabetes.

The quantity of food and drink you need if you have diabetes is influenced by your age, gender, degree of exercise, and the goals you wish to attain. A healthy diet emphasizes variety, with different meals from each major food type taken regularly.

And when we say "balanced," we're talking about eating more of certain items while eating less of others. However, as plates and bowls have gotten bigger, portion sizes have risen. Furthermore, larger doses may make maintaining a healthy weight more challenging. We offer a range of nutritious food recipes for you in this book that will benefit you.

1. Tips for Living a Better Journey on a Diabetic Lifestyle

Diabetes is not always easy. It can be difficult to balance out what you eat, how much you exercise, and the medications that your doctor prescribes. You may feel like it's impossible to know what's best for you and live an active lifestyle. However, there are numerous strategies to improve your health so that diabetes no longer holds you back.

These tips will help make a living with diabetes easier by giving you more control over your day-to-day life. Start today with these five things: drink water, get enough sleep, get regular checkups with your doctor, find support groups in your community, and manage stress. Try to do these things daily, and soon you'll be living a healthier life with diabetes.

A Journey Is Never Over

Diabetes isn't just an illness—it's also a lifestyle. It's something you live with day-to-day, so it's important to make your journey as easy as possible by taking control of your diabetes at home and managing your stress levels.

Water Is Key to Good Healthy Mindset

Remember that diabetes is something that you live with continually, so remember to drink water regularly throughout the day. Drink at least 64 ounces per day (approximately 4 liters).

Drink Water to Maintain a Healthy Mindset

Sleep is actually important for overall health, but it's even more important for your brain health. Sleep deprivation can have an impact on how your brain functions, so, if possible, try to get seven hours of sleep each night. Visit our site for tinnitus, tinnitus treatment, and tinnitus home treatment.

Stay Regular to Control Your Blood Sugar Levels

If your blood sugar levels are too high, your body will produce extra insulin to bring them back down. If your blood sugar levels are too low, your body doesn't create enough insulin to bring them up. Getting in the habit of checking your actual blood sugar levels at home and between doctor's appointments is the best way to let your body know what's normal and what's not is the best way to let your body know what's normal and what's not.

Some people find it helpful to carry a device around with them that records every time they check their blood sugar. This helps give them a baseline to tell if their doctor is over or under-reacting to their blood sugar variability.

Knowledge is power. The more you know about your body's reactions, the easier it will be to manage your condition. Even if you don't do anything else with the device, it can make you realize how much influence you have over your own health.

Eat To Live, Don't Live to Eat

Food is fuel—it gives you the energy to do everything in life that matters to you. But depending on what food choices you make, certain foods could put your health at risk. Remember, choosing to eat foods with little to no fat could help lower your risk for heart disease.

Eat Your Portions of Fruits and Vegetables

If you're looking for a balanced diet to start with, focus on fruits and vegetables. Try eating two cups of fruit and two cups of vegetables each day. Be sure to count your portions right—one cup of fruit is the size of your fist, while one cup of vegetables is the size of a baseball. If you're not actually sure how much that is, go measure them out at home!

Adding additional fruits and vegetables to your diet can also help you get more vitamins. However, each fruit or vegetable contains a different set of vitamins, so you should choose the right ones for your body.

Explore new ways to exercise with some of the new classes we offer at our Center. You can also choose from some of the classes we offer at other locations in your community.

Change Your Style of Life to Impact Your Blood Sugar Levels

Finding the right insulin to cover your lifestyle can be difficult. It may take some time to find one that suits you, so consult with a clinician and choose basal insulin that fits your needs.

Chapter 1: Breakfast Recipes

Recipe 1: Almond Quinoa with Cranberries

Serving Size: 4

Cooking Time: 20 minutes

Ingredients:

- 4 ounces slivered almonds
- 3/4 cup dry quinoa
- 3 tablespoons dried cranberries
- 1 tablespoon honey (or 1 tablespoon cinnamon sugar)

Directions:

1. Heat a large saucepan over medium-high heat. Add almonds and cook for approximately about 2 minutes or until beginning to lightly brown, stirring frequently. Set aside on separate plate.
2. Pour 1 1/2 cups water into the saucepan and bring to a boil, add the quinoa, reduce heat to low, cover and cook 13–15 minutes or until liquid is absorbed. Remove from actual heat and let stand, covered, for 5 minutes.
3. Top with the almonds and cranberries. Drizzle with the honey (or sprinkle with cinnamon sugar.)

Nutritional Value: Calories 330; Fat 16g; Carbohydrates 39g; Protein 11g

Recipe 2: Apple Spiced Overnight Oats

Serving Size: 2

Cooking Time: 10 minutes

Ingredients:

- ¼ cup hemp hearts
- 1 tbsp. chia seeds
- 3 tbsp. rolled oats
- ¼ cup plain Greek yogurt
- 1 tsp. cinnamon
- ¼ cup shredded apple
- 6-8 pecan halves
- ¾ cup milk

Directions:

1. Combine the oats, hemp hearts, chia seeds, and cinnamon in a mason jar.
2. Mix the Greek yogurt and shredded apple in the oats.
3. Stir in the milk until everything is completely mixed.
4. Allow the oats to cool in the refrigerator for about 2 hours.
5. Before serving, sprinkle with pecans.

Nutritional Value: Calories 278; Fat 19g; Carbohydrates 19g; Protein 15g

Recipe 3: Avocado and Goat Cheese Toast

Serving Size: 2

Cooking Time: 10 minutes

Ingredients:

- 2 slices whole-wheat thin-sliced bread
- ½ avocado
- 2 tablespoons crumbled goat cheese
- Salt to taste

Directions:

1. In a toaster or broiler, toast the bread until browned.
2. Remove the flesh from the avocado. In a large-sized bowl, use a fork to mash the avocado flesh. Spread it onto the toast.
3. Sprinkle with the goat cheese and season lightly with salt.
4. Add any toppings and serve.

Nutritional Value: Calories 137; Fat 6g; Carbohydrates 18g; Protein 5g

Recipe 4: Bagel with Poached Egg

Serving Size: 2

Cooking Time: 10 minutes

Ingredients:

- 2 bagels
- 1 large tomato
- 2 tbsp. basil pesto
- 2 eggs
- Salt and black pepper to taste
- ¼ Aubergine
- 1 tbsp. olive oil

Directions:

1. Tomato and Aubergine should be cut into slices. Each bagel should include 1-2 tomato slices and 1-2 Aubergine slices. Brush the prepared slices with some olive oil, place them on a baking sheet, and roast for 5 minutes at 350°F, flipping once.
2. Poach the two eggs in the pan. Spread 1 tbsp. basil pesto on each bagel. Under the grill, toast the bagels until the edges begin to brown. Place an egg on top of the Aubergine and tomato slices on the bagels. Enjoy!

Nutritional Value: Calories 361; Fat 4g; Carbohydrates 38g; Protein 17g

Recipe 5: Baked Eggs

Serving Size: 8

Cooking Time: 20 minutes

Ingredients:

- 1 cup water
- 2 tablespoons no-trans-fat tub margarine, melted
- 1 cup reduced-fat buttermilk baking mix
- 1½ cups fat-free cottage cheese
- 2 teaspoons chopped onion
- 1 teaspoon dried parsley
- ½ cup grated reduced-fat Cheddar cheese
- 1 egg, slightly beaten
- 1¼ cups egg substitute
- 1 cup fat-free milk

Directions:

1. Place the steam rack into the bottom of the inner pot and pour in 1 cup of water.
2. Grease a round springform pan that will fit into the inner pot of the Instant Pot.
3. Pour melted margarine into springform pan.
4. Mix together buttermilk baking mix, cottage cheese, onion, parsley, cheese, egg, egg substitute, and milk in large mixing bowl.
5. Pour mixture over melted margarine. Stir slightly to distribute margarine.
6. Place the springform large-sized pan onto the steam rack, close the lid, and secure to the locking position. Be sure the vent is turned to sealing. Set for 20 minutes on Manual at high pressure.
7. Let the pressure release naturally.
8. Carefully remove the springform pan with the handles of the steam rack and allow to stand 10 minutes before cutting and serving.

Nutritional Value: Calories 155; Fat 5g; Carbohydrates 15g; Protein 12g

Recipe 6: Banana Bread French Toast

Serving Size: 2

Cooking Time: 25 minutes

Ingredients:

- 8 slices banana bread,
- 2 tsp butter,
- 4 eggs
- ¾ cup low-fat milk
- 1 tsp vanilla extract
- ¼ tsp ground cinnamon
- Toasted hewed walnuts, sliced banana and maple syrup for topping

Directions:

1. In a 4-cup measuring cup or mixing dish, whisk the eggs, milk, vanilla, and cinnamon.
2. In a 9-by-13-inch baking dish, lay 4 pieces of banana bread. Pour half of the mixture over the bread. Soak for 1 minute, then flip the slices and soak for another minute.
3. Over medium heat, melt 1 tablespoon butter. Sauté the slices for 2 - 3 min. Per side, till browned. To keep warm, transfer to a platter and cover. Using the leftover banana bread, egg mixture, and butter, repeat the process.
4. Walnuts, sliced banana, and maple syrup can be sprinkled before serving.

Nutritional Value: Calories 294; Fat 11.4g; Carbohydrates 40.8g; Protein 8.6g

Recipe 7: Black Bean and Egg Tacos

Serving Size: 4

Cooking Time: 13 minutes

Ingredients:

- ½ cup red onion, diced
- 8 6-inch white soft corn tortillas, warmed
- 1 clove of garlic, minced
- 1 teaspoon of avocado oil
- ¼ cup chopped fresh cilantro
- 4 eggs
- 1- 15 oz can of black beans, rinsed and drained
- 1 small avocado, diced
- ¼ teaspoon of ground chipotle powder
- ½ cup fresh or your favorite jarred salsa

Directions:

1. Make scrambled eggs as you always do.
2. In a pan, heat the avocado oil. Add onions and sauté for 3 minutes until tender.
3. Add garlic and beans and cook for 2-5 minutes until heated through and shiny.
4. Toast the tortillas until a little tender.
5. Put aside and wrap in a cloth napkin to keep them warm.
6. On a tortilla, layer the beans and eggs. Top up the taco with salsa, avocado, and cilantro.

Nutritional Value: Calories 349; Fat 15g; Carbohydrates 12g; Protein 11g

Recipe 8: Brussels Sprout with Fried Eggs

Serving Size: 4

Cooking Time: 20 minutes

Ingredients:

- 3 teaspoons extra-virgin olive oil, divided
- 1 pound (454 g) Brussels sprouts, sliced
- 2 garlic cloves, thinly sliced
- 1/4 teaspoon salt
- Juice of 1 lemon
- 4 eggs

Directions:

1. Heat 11/2 teaspoons of olive oil in a large skillet over medium heat.
2. Add the Brussels sprouts and sauté for 6 to 8 minutes until crispy and tender, stirring frequently.
3. Stir in the garlic and cook for about 1 minute until fragrant. Sprinkle with the salt and lemon juice.
4. Remove from the large-sized skillet to a plate and set aside.
5. Heat the remaining oil in the large-sized skillet over medium-high heat. Crack the eggs one at a time into the skillet and fry for about 3 minutes. Flip the eggs and continue cooking, or until the egg whites are set and the yolks are cooked to your liking.
6. Serve the fried eggs over the crispy Brussels sprouts.
7. Tip: The Brussels sprouts, like other brassica vegetables, can be prepared ahead of time when you are free and kept in an airtight container in the refrigerator until ready to use.

Nutritional Value: Calories 157; Fat 8.9g; Carbohydrates 11.8g; Protein 10.1g

Recipe 9: Bulgur Porridge

Serving Size: 4

Cooking Time: 15 minutes

Ingredients:

- 4 cups 1% low-fat milk
- 1 cup bulgur
- ⅓ cup dried cherries
- ¼ tablespoon salt
- ⅓ cup dried apricots, coarsely chopped
- ½ cup sliced almonds

Directions:

1. Put the milk, bulgur, dried cherries, and salt in a large saucepan. Bring to a boil.
2. Reduce the heat and simmer while constantly stirring, until tender and oatmeal are tender for 10-15 minutes. Divide among 4 bowls.
3. Garnish with apricots and almonds and serve.

Nutritional Value: Calories 340; Fat 6.7g; Carbohydrates 18g; Protein 15g

Recipe 10: Cauliflower Cups

Serving Size: 12

Cooking Time: 30 minutes

Ingredients:

- 3 cups riced cauliflower
- ¾ cup mozzarella cheese
- 3 eggs
- ¼ cup milk
- 2 tbsp. parmesan cheese
- 1/8 tsp. salt

Directions:

1. Using nonstick cooking spray, coat the muffin pan.
2. Combine all ingredients (except parmesan cheese) in a big mixing bowl. Fill every muffin cup 2/3 full with batter using a cookie scoop. Parmesan cheese should be sprinkled on top of each cauliflower cup.
3. Preheat the oven to a heat of 350°F and bake for 30 minutes. While the cauliflower cups are still warm, enjoy them.

Nutritional Value: Calories 151; Fat 3g; Carbohydrates 2g; Protein 10g

Recipe 11: Cauliflower Fritters

Serving Size: 12

Cooking Time: 25 minutes

Ingredients:

- 1 large cauliflower
- ¼ cup almond flour
- 3 large eggs
- ½ cup white cheddar cheese, grated
- 1 tsp. garlic powder
- 2 tbsp. parmesan cheese, grated
- ½ tsp. pepper
- ½ tsp. salt
- 1 tbsp. olive oil
- green onions, garnish
- 4 tbsp. sour cream, for garnish

Directions:

1. Cut florets out of the cauliflower head. In a food processor, pulse cauliflower florets for several seconds till riced and no large bits remain. In a mixing dish, whisk together the eggs using a fork. Combine the cauliflower rice, cheeses, almond flour, salt, garlic powder, and pepper in a mixing bowl.
2. Mix everything together thoroughly, ensuring sure the egg is entirely incorporated. Allow approximately about 10 minutes for the mixture to rest. Heat a big nonstick pan over medium heat while the mixture rests. Add the olive oil once the pan is heated. Scoop a quarter cup of the cauliflower fritter batter into the pan. Flatten the fritter mixture with the back of a spatula or the bottom of a 1/4 cup, measuring until it is approximately 1/2 inch thick. The pan can hold roughly 2–3 fritters at a time.
3. Cook for approximately about 5–7 minutes on each side before flipping. It's important not to turn the fritters too soon since they're rather delicate while they're first frying. Remove the cooked fritters and lay them on a wire rack to drain any excess oil. As the fritters cool, they will become less delicate and crispier. Serve your fritters with a dollop of sour cream and some chopped green onions as a garnish.

Nutritional Value: Calories 186; Fat 6g; Carbohydrates 4g; Protein 5g

Recipe 12: Chicken Nacho Casserole

Serving Size: 1

Cooking Time: 25 minutes

Ingredients:

- 1 non-stick cooking spray
- 2 tsp. chili powder
- 1/2 tsp. cumin
- 1/2 tsp. garlic powder
- 2/3 cup cheddar cheese (reduced-fat, shredded)
- 1/8 tsp. black pepper
- 1 lb. chicken breasts (boneless, skinless, cut into small pieces)
- 1 can fire-roasted tomatoes (15 oz., diced)
- 1 cup black beans (no salt added, drained and rinsed)
- 1 1/2 oz. baked tortilla chips (crushed, (or about 24)

Directions:

1. Preheat the oven to 375°F.
2. Use cooking spray to spray a 2 1/2 qt. baking dish.
3. Season the chicken with black pepper.
4. Use cooking spray to spray a large sauté pan and heat over medium-high.
5. Add the chicken. Then cook for about 8 minutes.
6. Add the black beans, diced tomatoes, chili powder, garlic powder, and cumin to the pan.
7. Reduce the heat to low. Then simmer for about 5 minutes.
8. Pour the prepared chicken mixture into the baking dish.
9. Sprinkle cheese on top. Then top with the crushed tortilla chips.
10. Bake until the cheese is melted for about 12 minutes.

Nutritional Value: Calories 210; Fat 6g; Carbohydrates 25g; Protein 23g

Recipe 13: Egg and Ham Burrito

Serving Size: 3

Cooking Time: 13 minutes

Ingredients:

- 4 eggs
- Egg whites
- 1 dash of hot pepper sauce
- ¼ teaspoon of black pepper
- 2 tablespoons cheddar cheese
- 2 tablespoons margarine
- 4 slices of deli
- ¼ cup sliced onion
- ¼ cup diced green pepper.
- 4 heated corn tortillas
- Salsa

Directions:

1. Mix eggs, egg whites, whole poivrade, black pepper, and cheese with a medium base.
2. Add the spread to a medium non-stick pan on a medium flame.
3. Add the ham and fry for 2-3 minutes. Remove the ham from the pan.
4. Add the onion and fresh pepper to a new pan and cook for about five minutes. Add the ham back to the pan.
5. Raise again and add the eggs to the pan.
6. Carefully roll the eggs with a spoon or spatula and slowly change state over low heat until the egg boils and hardens.
7. Divide the egg mixture evenly into four portions.
8. Pour each part of the egg mixture into the dough and add a teaspoon of salsa. Fold the cake to break.

Nutritional Value: Calories 210; Fat 3g; Carbohydrates 10g; Protein 6g

Recipe 14: Egg and Spinach Breakfast Burritos

Serving Size: 10

Cooking Time: 30 minutes

Ingredients:

- 1-pound bulk thin turkey breakfast sausage
- 1 tsp canola oil
- 1 cup frozen cubed hash brown potatoes, hewed
- 1 small red onion, hewed
- 1 small sweet red pepper, hewed
- 6 cups (about 4 oz.) fresh spinach, coarsely hewed
- 6 large eggs, beaten
- 10 multigrain tortillas (8 inches), warmed
- 3/4 cup crumbled queso fresco or feta cheese
- Guacamole and salsa, optional

Directions:

1. Cook sausage in a large frying pan
2. Heat oil in the same pan. Cook for 5-7 minutes, occasionally turning, until potatoes, onion, and pepper gets soft, Stir in the spinach for 1-2 minutes, or until it has wilted. Cook, stir the sausage and eggs until no liquid egg remains.
3. Spread 1/2 cup filling over each tortilla's middle and top with cheese. Fold the bottom and edges of the rollover the filling and roll it up. Serve with guacamole and salsa, if preferred.
4. Freeze option: Before preparing burritos, cool the filling. Burritos should be individually wrapped in foil and frozen in a sealed plastic freezer bag. Freeze for up to a month in the freezer. Thaw partly overnight in the refrigerated or colder before using. Prepare a medium-heat campfire or grill. Wrap the prepared burritos in foil and place them on a grill grate over a campfire or on a grill. Grill for 25-30 minutes, rotating periodically, until well heated.

Nutritional Value: Calories 333; Fat 15g; Carbohydrates 27g; Protein 22g

Recipe 15: Feta Scrambled Egg Wraps

Serving Size: 4

Cooking Time: 15 minutes

Ingredients:

- 1-1/2 cups egg
- 3/4 cup smashed feta cheese
- 2 tsp sliced pepperoncini, hewed
- 4 warmed wheat tortillas (8 inches)

Directions:

1. Preheat a large-sized nonstick skillet over medium heat.
2. Pour in the egg replacement and heat, constantly stirring, until the mixture thickens and no liquid egg remains.
3. Heat through gently stirring in cheese and pepperoncini.
4. Toss in tortillas and serve.

Nutritional Value: Calories 239; Fat 6g; Carbohydrates 7g; Protein 17g

Recipe 16: Honey French Toast

Serving Size: 6

Cooking Time: 10 minutes

Ingredients:

- 1 cup low-fat milk
- 4 large eggs
- 1 tbsp. honey
- 1/8 tsp. pepper
- ½ tsp. ground cinnamon
- 12 slices whole wheat bread
- vanilla frosting or Cinnamon sugar (optional)

Directions:

1. Whisk together the eggs, honey, milk, pepper, and cinnamon in a small bowl.
2. Both sides of the bread should actually be dipped in the egg mixture.
3. Cook 3-4 minutes per side on a greased hot griddle, or until golden brown.
4. Top with vanilla icing or sprinkle with cinnamon sugar, if preferred.

Nutritional Value: Calories 218; Fat 6g; Carbohydrates 28g; Protein 13g

Recipe 17: Mushroom Breakfast Burrito

Serving Size: 1

Cooking Time: 20 minutes

Ingredients:

- 1/2 tbsp. neutral oil canola, vegetable, grapeseed
- 1/8 white onion diced
- 1/2 garlic clove minced
- 1/2 cups Cremini mushrooms chopped
- Cooking spray
- 1 large whole wheat tortillas
- 2/3 cup + 2 tbsp. goat cheese
- 1 cup loosely packed spinach chopped
- 2/3 tsp. salt
- 2 large eggs
- 3/4 tbsp. milk
- Salt and pepper to taste

Directions:

1. Add oil to the pan in a large skillet over medium-high heat. Add the garlic, onion and cook until translucent, for about 2 to 3 minutes. Add the mushrooms, then cook for 3 minutes until they are golden brown. Flip the mushrooms to allow the other side to cook.
2. In the pan, place spinach and cook for about 3 to 4 minutes until it's wilted. Season with prepared salt and stir all the veggies together. Remove from the actual heat, then set it aside.
3. Whisk together the prepared milk and eggs in a large bowl. Season with pepper and salt to taste. Over medium heat, heat another large skillet, spray the skillet using cooking spray. Add egg mixture, then cook until the eggs have set, frequently stirring, for about 4 to 5 minutes. Remove from heat.
4. In the microwave, heat the tortillas for 10 seconds. On a piece of aluminum foil, lay out the tortillas and spread half tbsp. of goat cheese on it. Distribute the roasted vegetables and scrambled eggs evenly. Roll up in the foil and place it in a freezer bag. Then freeze.
5. Unwrap the burritos from the foil when ready to eat from the freezer. Serve and enjoy.

Nutritional Value: Calories 385; Fat 20g; Carbohydrates 6g; Protein 20g

Recipe 18: Omelet with Turmeric

Serving Size: 2

Cooking Time: 15 minutes

Ingredients:

- 4 large eggs
- Kosher salt
- 1 tablespoon olive oil
- 1 quarter teaspoon brown mustard seeds turmeric powder
- 2 green onions, finely chopped
- ¼ cup diced plum tomato
- Dash of black pepper

Directions:

1. Whisk the eggs and salt together.
2. In a large-sized pan, heat oil over medium heat.
3. Use mustard and turmeric seeds. Stir constantly for approximately about 30 seconds or until the seeds crackled.
4. Add the onions and cook for 30 seconds or until tender, stirring constantly. Add the tomatoes. Cook for 1 minute until very tender.
5. Pour the bowl with the egg mixture. Spread evenly. Cook until the actual edges of the eggs are set.
6. Slide the edges of the spatula between the edges of the omelet and the plate. Carefully lift the edges of the omelet by tilting the pan so that it comes in contact with the egg mixture— the same procedure from the opposite edge.
7. Continue cooking until the setting is ready. Loosen the omelet and fold it in half with a spatula. Carefully slide the omelet onto the plate. Cut the omelet in half and sprinkle with pepper.

Nutritional Value: Calories 216; Fat 16.9g; Carbohydrates 14g; Protein 13.3g

Recipe 19: Parmesan Herb Frittata

Serving Size: 8

Cooking Time: 20 minutes

Ingredients:

- 1 tbsp. olive oil
- 1 tbsp. garlic, minced
- ½ onion, diced
- ½ cup milk of choice
- 8 eggs
- ½ tsp. dried oregano
- ¾ tsp. salt
- ¼ tsp. black pepper
- ¼ tsp. cayenne pepper
- 2 tbsp. fresh parsley, chopped
- ¾ cup low-fat mozzarella, shredded
- ½ tsp. dried basil
- 2 roasted red peppers, jarred
- ¾ cup grated parmesan
- ¼ tsp. ground mustard

Directions:

1. Preheat the oven to 425°F. On medium-high heat, add the prepared olive oil to a cast iron skillet. Once the oil is heated, add the chopped onion. Stir with a spatula while it cooks.
2. Sauté until the onions are nearly tender. Then add the prepared minced garlic to the skillet and sauté for about one minute or until golden. Whisk together the milk, eggs, oregano, salt, cayenne pepper, basil, black pepper, and ground mustard in a separate bowl. Turn off the heat when the garlic and onion are done. Distribute evenly across the bottom of the skillet. Prepare the canned roasted red peppers by dicing them. Spread the red pepper in the skillet as well.
3. On the top layer are parmesan cheese, mozzarella cheese, and fresh parsley. Over everything, pour the egg mixture. Bake it for 16 to 20 minutes, or until the middle is barely set. Check to ensure that the center is not too wiggly before removing it from the oven. Allow a few minutes before serving. While the frittata bubbles vigorously in the oven, it will calm down as it cools.

Nutritional Value: Calories 167; Fat 12g; Carbohydrates 3g; Protein 12g

Recipe 20: Parsley Chicken Breast

Serving Size: 4

Cooking Time: 40 minutes

Ingredients:

- 1 tablespoon dry parsley
- 1 tablespoon dry basil
- 4 chicken breast halves, boneless and skinless
- 1/2 teaspoon salt
- 1/2 teaspoon red pepper flakes, crushed
- 2 tomatoes, sliced

Directions:

1. Preheat your oven to 350 degrees F
2. Take a prepared 9x13 inch baking dish and grease it up with cooking spray
3. Sprinkle 1 tablespoon of parsley, 1 teaspoon of basil and spread the mixture over your baking dish
4. Arrange the chicken breast halves over the dish and sprinkle garlic slices on top
5. Take a small bowl and add 1 teaspoon parsley, 1 teaspoon of basil, salt, basil, red pepper and mix well. Pour the mixture over the chicken breast
6. Top with tomato slices and cover, bake for 25 minutes
7. Remove the cover and bake for 15 minutes more
8. Serve and enjoy!

Nutritional Value: Calories 150; Fat 4g; Carbohydrates 4g; Protein 25g

Recipe 21: Potato-Bacon Gratin

Serving Size: 8

Cooking Time: 20 minutes

Ingredients:

- 1 tablespoon olive oil
- 1 (6-ounce / 170-g) bag fresh spinach
- 1 clove garlic, minced
- 4 large potatoes, peeled or unpeeled, divided
- 6 ounces (170 g) Canadian bacon slices, divided
- 5 ounces (142 g) reduced-fat grated Swiss Cheddar, divided
- 1 cup lower-sodium, lower-fat chicken broth

Directions:

1. Set the prepared Instant Pot to Sauté and pour in the olive oil. Cook the prepared spinach and garlic in olive oil just until spinach is wilted (5 minutes or less). Turn off the instant pot.
2. Cut potatoes into thin slices about ¼ inch thick.
3. In a springform large-sized pan that will fit into the inner pot of your Instant Pot, spray it with nonstick spray then layer ⅓ the potatoes, half the bacon, ⅓ the cheese, and half the wilted spinach.
4. Repeat layers ending with potatoes. Reserve ⅓ cheese for later.
5. Pour chicken broth over all.
6. Wipe the bottom of your Instant Pot to soak up any remaining oil, then add in 2 cups of water and the steam rack. Place the springform pan on top.
7. Close the lid and secure to the locking position. Be sure the vent is turned to sealing. Set for 35 minutes on Manual at high pressure.
8. Perform a quick release.
9. Top with the remaining cheese, then allow to stand 10 minutes before removing from the Instant Pot, cutting and serving.

Nutritional Value: Calories 220; Fat 7g; Carbohydrates 28g; Protein 14g

Recipe 22: Pumpkin Pancakes

Serving Size: 3

Cooking Time: 10 minutes

Ingredients:

- ½ cup oats
- 1 oz. pumpkin puree
- 2 egg whites
- 1 scoop protein powder
- 2 tsp. stevia
- ½ tsp. cinnamon
- Cooking spray
- Apple, for serving
- Sugar-free syrup for serving

Directions:

1. In a blender, combine oats, egg whites, pumpkin puree, protein powder, cinnamon, and stevia. Blend until completely smooth.
2. Place a large-sized pan over medium-high heat and coat it with cooking spray. Pour 1/3 of the batter onto the pan and equally distribute it. Allow the pancake to cook for approximately 2 minutes, or until the edges are lightly golden, before turning it and continuing to cook for another 2 minutes.
3. Place the pancake on a platter and put it aside while you finish the other two pancakes. Enjoy with sugar-free syrup and apple slices.

Nutritional Value: Calories 182; Fat 1g; Carbohydrates 16g; Protein 22g

Recipe 23: Quinoa Burrito

Serving Size: 1

Cooking Time: 10 minutes

Ingredients:

- 1 cup quinoa
- 2 cups black beans
- 4 finely chopped onions, green
- 4 bulbs of finely chopped garlic
- 2 freshly cut limes
- 1 big tablespoon cumin
- 2 beautifully diced avocado
- 1 small cup beautifully diced cilantro

Directions:

1. Boil quinoa as per instructions.
2. Heat beans over low heat.
3. Add other ingredients to the beans pot and let it mix well for about 15 minutes.
4. Serve quinoa and add the prepared beans on top.

Nutritional Value: Calories 117; Fat 8g; Carbohydrates 22g; Protein 27g

Recipe 24: Sausage Tortilla Breakfast Bake

Serving Size: 6

Cooking Time: 50 minutes

Ingredients:

- 8 oz. lean sausage
- 1/2 cup canned diced tomatoes and green chilies
- 6 corn tortillas (6 inches)
- 1/2 cup shredded cheese
- 1/4 cup shredded cheese
- 2 green chopped onions,
- 6 large eggs
- 3/4 cup fat-free milk
- 3/4 tsp paprika
- 1/4 tsp ground cumin
- Reduced-fat sour cream, optional

Directions:

1. Preheat the oven to 350 degrees Fahrenheit. Cook and shred sausage in a large pan over medium heat for 4-6 minutes, or until no longer pink. Toss in the tomatoes.
2. Lightly grease a 9-inch deep-dish pie pan. Use partial tortillas to line the pie dish, and the remaining sausage mixture, green onion and cheeses will be sprinkled on top. repeat the layer
3. Whisk together eggs, milk, paprika, and cumin in a mixing dish; pour gently over layers. Bake for 25-30 minutes, uncovered, until set. Allow for a 10-minute rest period. Cut the wedges in half. Serve with sour cream, salsa, and more green onions, if preferred.

Nutritional Value: Calories 268; Fat 14g; Carbohydrates 14g; Protein 22g

Recipe 25: Savory Egg Muffins

Serving Size: 6

Cooking Time: 33 minutes

Ingredients:

- 1 ½ cups of water
- 2 tablespoons unsalted butter
- 1 6 oz package stove, top lower-sodium stuffing mix for chicken
- 3 oz bulk pork sausage
- Cooking spray
- 6 eggs, beaten
- ½ cup (1.5 oz) Monterey Jack cheese, shredded
- ½ cup finely chopped red bell pepper
- ¼ cup of sliced green onions

Directions:

1. Preheat the oven to 400°F.
2. Boil 1½ cups of water and the butter. Mix the ingredients. Cover, remove from heat and let stand for 5 minutes.
3. Use a spoon to fluff the filling. Leave it for 10 minutes.
4. Cook the sausages in a small skillet over medium heat until they brown and cool. Stir to break.
5. Press about ¼ cup into the bottom and sides of 12 oil-coated muffin cups.
6. Pour in eggs equal to cups of filling. Top the eggs evenly with cheese, ham, peppers, and green onions if desired.
7. Bake the muffins at 400°F for 18-20 minutes.
8. Let stand 5 minutes before eating. Loosen the glass muffin with a thin, sharp knife along the edge.
9. Remove from the casserole dish. Serve immediately.

Nutritional Value: Calories 292; Fat 16.7g; Carbohydrates 12g; Protein 14.6g

Recipe 26: Scrambled Yellow Tofu

Serving Size: 4

Cooking Time: 15 minutes

Ingredients:

- 1 cup crumbled serving of tofu
- 1 small cup finely chopped onions
- 1 teaspoon the fresh parsley
- 1 teaspoon coconut oil
- 1 cup soft spinach
- 1 small teaspoon turmeric
- 2 avocados
- 75g of tomatoes
- 1 small spoon of roasted paprika

Directions:

1. Make tofu crumbs with your hands and keep them aside in a bowl.
2. In a pan, sauté diced onions in oil till it softens.
3. Put your tofu, tomatoes, and other seasonings in a pan and mix well until combine till tofu is well prepared.
4. Add veggies to it and stir.
5. Serve in a bowl alongside some avocado and fresh salad.

Nutritional Value: Calories 191; Fat 3g; Carbohydrates 3g; Protein 30g

Recipe 27: Spicy Jalapeno Popper Deviled Eggs

Serving Size: 4

Cooking Time: 10 minutes

Ingredients:

- 4 large whole eggs, hardboiled
- 2 tablespoons Keto-Friendly mayonnaise
- ¼ cup cheddar cheese, grated
- 2 slices bacon, cooked and crumbled
- 1 jalapeno, sliced

Directions:

1. Cut eggs in half, remove the yolk and put them in bowl
2. Lay egg whites on a platter
3. Mix in remaining ingredients and mash them with the egg yolks
4. Transfer yolk mix back to the egg whites
5. Serve and enjoy!

Nutritional Value: Calories 176; Fat 14g; Carbohydrates 0.7g; Protein 10g

Recipe 28: Sweet Potato Hash

Serving Size: 4

Cooking Time: 10 minutes

Ingredients:

- 2 large sweet potatoes, cubes
- 1 small bell pepper, chopped
- 2 tbsp. olive oil
- ½ tsp. kosher salt
- 1 tsp. smoked paprika
- 5 scallions, thinly sliced
- 1 tbsp. pickled jalapeños, chopped
- 1 tbsp. fresh parsley, chopped

Directions:

1. In a microwave-safe dish, combine 2 tbsp. of water with the sweet potatoes. Cover and microwave on high for approximately about 10 minutes, or until fork-tender sweet potatoes.
2. In a large skillet, heat the oil over medium-high heat. Add the sweet potatoes, smoked paprika, bell pepper, and salt once the pan is heated. Cook, occasionally stirring, for approximately 5 minutes, or until the sweet potatoes have browned. Cook for approximately about another 2 minutes after adding the pickled jalapenos and scallions.
3. Garnish with fresh parsley and divide among 4 serving dishes.

Nutritional Value: Calories 225; Fat 7g; Carbohydrates 39g; Protein 4g

Recipe 29: Walnut and Oat Granola

Serving Size: 16

Cooking Time: 30 minutes

Ingredients:

- 4 cups rolled oats
- 1 cup walnut pieces
- ½ cup pepitas
- ¼ teaspoon salt
- 1 teaspoon ground cinnamon
- 1 teaspoon ground ginger
- ½ cup coconut oil, melted
- ½ cup unsweetened applesauce
- 1 teaspoon vanilla extract
- ½ cup dried cherries

Directions:

1. Preheat the oven to a heat of 350°F (180°C). Line a baking sheet with parchment paper.
2. In a large bowl, toss the oats, walnuts, pepitas, salt, cinnamon, and ginger.
3. In a large measuring cup, combine the coconut oil, applesauce, and vanilla. Pour over the dry mixture and mix well.
4. Transfer the prepared mixture to the prepared baking sheet. Cook for 30 minutes, stirring about halfway through. Remove from the oven and let the granola sit undisturbed until completely cool. Break the granola into pieces, and stir in the dried cherries.
5. Transfer to an airtight container, and store at room temperature for up to 2 weeks.

Nutritional Value: Calories 225; Fat 14.9g; Carbohydrates 20.1g; Protein 4.9g

Recipe 30: Zucchini and Yellow Pepper Scramble

Serving Size: 4

Cooking Time: 10 minutes

Ingredients:

- 1 tsp olive oil
- 1 spring onion, diced
- ½ yellow bell pepper, cut into cubes
- ½ zucchini, cut into cubes
- 8 large eggs, beaten
- 1 tomato, seeded and cut into cubes
- 2 tsp fresh oregano, diced finely
- Himalayan pink salt, ground
- Black pepper, ground

Directions:

1. Heat a heavy bottom large-sized pan over medium heat and add the olive oil and cook until hot.
2. Toss in the diced spring onion, cubed yellow bell pepper, and the cubed zucchini, fry for 5 minutes until tender.
3. Add the prepared beaten eggs and using a spatula or fork, scramble the egg mixture for 5 minutes or until the eggs are cooked through.
4. Remove the large-sized pan off the heat and add the cubed tomato and diced oregano, mix to combine.
5. Season with ground Himalayan pink salt and ground black pepper and serve warm.

Nutritional Value: Calories 196; Fat 11g; Carbohydrates 6g; Protein 13g

Chapter 2: Lunch Recipes

Recipe 31: Baked Penne Pasta

Serving Size: 8

Cooking Time: 1 hour 10 minutes

Ingredients:

- 1/2 cup of breadcrumbs
- 1 tbsp of extra-virgin olive oil
- 2 small zucchinis
- 1 eggplant
- 1 green bell pepper
- 1 onion
- 1 stalk celery
- 1 garlic clove
- 1/4 cup of white wine
- 28 oz of tomatoes
- Pepper to taste
- Salt to taste
- 16 oz of penne rigatoni
- 2 cups of mozzarella cheese
- 2 eggs
- 2 tbsp of parmesan cheese

Directions:

1. Preheat the oven to 375 °F. Using a nonstick spray, coat a baking dish. Using some breadcrumbs, coat the dish and tap out the excess. Bring a large-sized saucepan of water to a boil for the pasta.
2. In a large-sized saucepan, heat the oil over medium-high heat. Cook, occasionally turning, until zucchini, eggplant, bell pepper, onion, and celery are soft, about 10 minutes. Cook for 1 minute more, stirring constantly. Stir in the wine for about 2 minutes until it has nearly completely evaporated. Toss in the tomatoes and the liquid. Cook, occasionally stirring, until the actual sauce has thickened, about 10-15 minutes. Add salt and pepper to taste. Allow cooling to actual room temperature in a large bowl.
3. Meanwhile, cook penne until done in boiling salted water. Drain and rinse thoroughly. Toss the spaghetti with the vegetables and add the mozzarella. Drizzle the eggs equally over the top of the pasta mixture in the prepared baking dish. Combine the remaining cup of breadcrumbs and Parmesan in a small bowl. Sprinkle over the top in an equal layer.
4. Bake pasta for 40-50 minutes, until brown and bubbling. Allow for approximately about a 10-minute rest period before serving.

Nutritional Value: Calories 372; Fat 18.3g; Carbohydrates 57.4g; Protein 18.3g

Recipe 32: Beef and Mushroom Casserole

Serving Size: 4

Cooking Time: 15 minutes

Ingredients:

- 1 tbsp olive oil
- 1 lb. rib eye steak, thinly sliced
- 1 onion, thinly sliced
- 8 oz mushrooms, sliced
- ¼ cup brandy or dry white wine
- ¾ cup beef stock
- 1 tsp whole-grain mustard
- ½ cup sour cream
- Himalayan pink salt, ground
- Black pepper, ground
- ¼ cup parsley, roughly chopped

Directions:

1. Heat the prepared olive oil in a large heavy bottom pan over high heat until hot.
2. Add the steak and fry for 2 to 3 minutes on each side, until semi-cooked through. Place into a dish.
3. Cook the sliced onion and sliced mushrooms for 5 minutes, until tender.
4. Carefully add the brandy or white wine to deglaze the pan, scraping up the browned bits from the bottom. Cook for approximately about 1 minute for the alcohol to evaporate.
5. Add the beef stock and whole-grain mustard and bring to a simmer, cook for 2 to 3 minutes, until reduced.
6. Return the beef to the pan and cook for 2 to 3 minutes.
7. Remove the large-sized pan from the heat and stir in the sour cream. Season with ground Himalayan pink salt and ground black pepper.
8. Place the cooked beef and mushrooms onto a serving dish, and sprinkle with the chopped parsley.

Nutritional Value: Calories 328; Fat 20g; Carbohydrates 8g; Protein 28g

Recipe 33: Butter Beef and Spinach

Serving Size: 4

Cooking Time: 10 minutes

Ingredients:

- 1 pound 85% lean ground beef
- 1 cup Water
- 4 cups Fresh spinach
- 3/4 tsp. Salt
- 1/4 cup Butter
- 1/4 tsp. Pepper
- 1/4 tsp. Garlic powder

Directions:

2. Brown the beef on Sauté in the Instant Pot.
3. Remove into a bowl. Drain grease and clean the pot.
4. Add water into the pot and place steam rack.
5. Place the bowl with the beef on top.
6. Add garlic powder, pepper, butter, salt, and spinach.
7. Cover with a foil and close the lid.
8. Press Manual and cook 2 minutes on High.
9. Do a quick release.
10. Remove foil, stir and serve.

Nutritional Value: Calories 272; Fat 19g; Carbohydrates 1g; Protein 18g

Recipe 34: Buttery Lemon Chicken

Serving Size: 4

Cooking Time: 10 minutes

Ingredients:

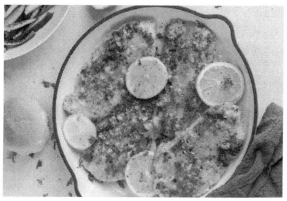

- 2 tablespoons margarine
- 1 medium onion, chopped
- 4 cloves garlic, minced
- ½ teaspoon paprika
- ½ teaspoon pepper
- 1 teaspoon dried parsley, or 1 tablespoon chopped fresh parsley
- 2 pounds (907 g) boneless chicken breasts or thighs
- ½ cup low-sodium chicken broth
- ⅓ cup lemon juice
- 1 teaspoon salt
- 1 to 2 tablespoons cornstarch
- 1 tablespoon water

Directions:

1. Set the Instant Pot to Sauté. When it is hot, add margarine to the inner pot and melt.
2. Add the onion, garlic, paprika, pepper, and parsley to melted margarine and sauté until onion starts to soften. Push onion to side of pot.
3. With the Instant Pot still at Sauté, add the chicken and sear on each side 3 to 5 minutes.
4. Mix broth, lemon juice, and salt together. Pour over chicken and stir to mix together.
5. Put on lid and set Instant Pot, move vent to sealing, and press Poultry. Set cook time for 7 minutes. Let depressurize naturally.
6. Remove chicken, leaving sauce in pot. Mix cornstarch in water and add to sauce. (Can start with 1 tablespoon cornstarch, and use second one if sauce isn't thick enough.)

Nutritional Value: Calories 350; Fat 12g; Carbohydrates 6g; Protein 52g

Recipe 35: Buttery Pot Roast

Serving Size: 4

Cooking Time: 1 hour 30 minutes

Ingredients:

- 4 tsp. Onion powder
- 2 tsp. Dried parsley
- 1 tsp. Salt
- 1 tsp. Garlic powder
- 1/2 tsp. Dried oregano
- 1/2 tsp. Pepper
- 1 (2-pound) Chuck roast
- 1 Tbsp. Coconut oil
- 1 cup Beef broth
- 1/2 packet Dry ranch seasoning
- 1 stick Butter
- 10 Pepperoncini

Directions:

1. Press Sauté and heat the Pot.
2. In a bowl, mix pepper, oregano, garlic powder, salt, parsley, and onion powder.
3. Rub seasoning onto the roast. Add oil the pot and place roast. Sear 5 minutes on each side.
4. Remove roast and set aside.
5. Add broth and deglaze. Place roast back into the Instant Pot. Sprinkle with ranch powder.
6. Place butter on top and add pepperoncini.
7. Close the lid and press Manual. Cook 90 minutes.
8. Do a natural release. Remove lid and remove roast.
9. Slice and serve.

Nutritional Value: Calories 561; Fat 33g; Carbohydrates 51g; Protein 5g

Recipe 36: Cabbage and Meat Gravy

Serving Size: 4

Cooking Time: 20 minutes

Ingredients:

- 1 tsp. olive oil
- 1 clove garlic, minced
- 1 small onion, chopped
- 3 cups chopped cabbage
- 14.5 oz. can diced tomatoes
- 1 lb. lean ground beef
- ¼ tsp. cinnamon
- 8 oz. low carb marinara
- ¼ tsp. salt

Directions:

1. Heat the oil in a large-sized pan, then add the onions and cook for 2-3 minutes. Garlic and ground meat should be added at this point.
2. Brown the ground beef in a skillet, then drain the fat before adding the tomatoes, marinara, and spices. Stir in the cabbage until everything is well combined.
3. Bring to a low hot boil, and then reduce to a low heat and cover.
4. Cook it for 15-20 minutes, or until the cabbage is tender. Serve without rice for a low-carb supper, or with rice for a family-friendly meal.

Nutritional Value: Calories 280; Fat 12g; Carbohydrates 16g; Protein 26g

Recipe 37: Cheesy Beef and Broccoli

Serving Size: 4

Cooking Time: 10 minutes

Ingredients:

- 1 pound 85% lean ground beef
- 1 tsp. salt
- 1/2 tsp. garlic powder
- 1/2 tsp. dried parsley
- 1/4 tsp. dried oregano
- 2 tbsp. butter
- 3/4 cup beef broth
- 2 cups broccoli florets
- 1/4 cup heavy cream
- 1 cup shredded cheddar cheese

Directions:

1. Brown the beef on Sauté in the Instant Pot.
2. Press Cancel and sprinkle seasonings over meat.
3. Add broccoli, broth, and butter. Close the lid.
4. Press Manual and cook for 2 minutes on High.
5. When done, press Cancel and stir in cheddar and heavy cream.
6. Serve.

Nutritional Value: Calories 476; Fat 33g; Carbohydrates 3g; Protein 30g

Recipe 38: Chicken Casablanca

Serving Size: 8

Cooking Time: 20 minutes

Ingredients:

- 2 large onions, sliced
- 1 teaspoon ground ginger
- 3 garlic cloves, minced
- 2 tablespoons canola oil, divided
- 3 pounds (1.4 kg) skinless chicken pieces
- 3 large carrots, diced
- 2 large potatoes, unpeeled, diced
- ½ teaspoon ground cumin
- ½ teaspoon salt
- ½ teaspoon pepper
- ¼ teaspoon cinnamon
- 2 tablespoons raisins
- 1 (14½-ounce / 411-g) can chopped tomatoes
- 3 small zucchini, sliced
- 1 (15-ounce / 425-g) can garbanzo beans, drained
- 2 tablespoons chopped parsley

Directions:

1. Using the Sauté function of the Instant Pot, cook the onions, ginger, and garlic in 1 tablespoon of the oil for 5 minutes, stirring constantly. Remove onions, ginger, and garlic from pot and set aside.
2. Brown the chicken pieces with the remaining oil, then add the cooked onions, ginger and garlic back in as well as all of the remaining ingredients, except the parsley.
3. Secure the cover lid and make sure vent is in the sealing position. Cook on Manual mode for 12 minutes.
4. When cook time is actually up, let the pressure release naturally for 5 minutes and then release the rest of the pressure manually.

Nutritional Value: Calories 395; Fat 10g; Carbohydrates 40g; Protein 36g

Recipe 39: Chicken Ricotta

Serving Size: 4

Cooking Time: 15 minutes

Ingredients:

- 1 lb. chicken tenders
- 1 tbsp. olive oil
- ½ cup parmesan cheese
- 1 cup ricotta cheese
- 1 cup cherry tomatoes, roasted
- 1 tsp. oregano, crushed
- Spiralized yellow squash, lightly sautéed
- olives, garnish optional

Directions:

1. Sauté chicken tenders with olive oil in a skillet. Parmesan, Ricotta, and oregano are combined in a small bowl.
2. To blend, stir everything together. Spirals of yellow squash should be combined with olive oil and season with salt and pepper to taste.
3. To assemble, spread ricotta cheese mixture over chicken tenders and top with roasted tomatoes.
4. To heat, place under the broiler. Serve with Squash mixture.

Nutritional Value: Calories 271; Fat 11g; Carbohydrates 5g; Protein 36g

Recipe 40: Crispy Dill Salmon

Serving Size: 4

Cooking Time: 15 minutes

Ingredients:

- 1 cup panko bread crumbs
- 2 tablespoons olive oil
- 2 tablespoons snipped fresh dill
- 1/4 teaspoon salt
- 1/8 teaspoon pepper
- 4 Salmon fillets (6 ounces each)
- 1 tablespoon lemon juice
- Lemon wedges

Directions:

1. Preheat the oven to 400 °. Mix the first 5 ingredients.
2. Place the salmon in a 15 x 10 x 1-inch container. Baking dish covered with cooking spray; Brush with lemon juice. Top with breadcrumb mixture, pat to stick.
3. Bake uncovered on an upper rack of the oven until fish flakes easily with a fork, 12 to 15 minutes. Serve with lemon wedges.

Nutritional Value: Calories 408; Fat 19.5g; Carbohydrates 20.6g; Protein 38.5g

Recipe 41: Feta and Sun-Dried Tomatoes Prawns

Serving Size: 4

Cooking Time: 30 minutes

Ingredients:

- 3 whole tomatoes, chopped
- ½ cup sun-dried tomatoes, chopped
- 2 tsp garlic, crushed
- 2 tsp avocado oil
- 1 tsp oregano, chopped
- Black pepper, ground
- Sea salt, ground
- 1½ lb. (16–20) prawn tails, deshelled and deveined
- 4 tsp lemon juice
- ½ cup ricotta cheese, crumbled

Directions:

1. Heat the oven to 450°F gas mark 8.
2. In a medium mixing bowl, add the chopped tomatoes, chopped sun-dried tomatoes, crushed garlic, avocado oil, chopped oregano, and mix until combined. Season with ground black pepper and ground sea salt.
3. Place the tomato mixture in an ovenproof baking dish.
4. Bake for 15 minutes until softened.
5. Mix in the deshelled prawn tails and lemon juice into the hot tomato mixture and top evenly with crumbled ricotta.
6. Bake for a approximately about a further 15 minutes until the prawns are fully cooked.

Nutritional Value: Calories 306; Fat 11g; Carbohydrates 12g; Protein 39g

Recipe 42: Garlic Galore Rotisserie Chicken

Serving Size: 4

Cooking Time: 10 minutes

Ingredients:

- 3 pounds (1.4 kg) whole chicken
- 2 tablespoons olive oil, divided
- Salt, to taste
- Pepper, to taste
- 20 to 30 cloves fresh garlic, peeled and left whole
- 1 cup low-sodium chicken stock, broth, or water
- 2 tablespoons garlic powder
- 2 teaspoons onion powder
- ½ teaspoon basil
- ½ teaspoon cumin
- ½ teaspoon chili powder

Directions:

1. Rub chicken with one tablespoon of the olive oil and sprinkle with salt and pepper.
2. Place the garlic cloves inside the chicken. Use butcher's twine to secure the legs.
3. Press the Sauté button on the Instant Pot, then add the rest of the olive oil to the inner pot.
4. When the pot is hot, place the chicken inside. You are just trying to sear it, so leave it for about 4 minutes on each side. Remove the chicken and set aside. Place the prepared trivet at the bottom of the inner pot and pour in the chicken stock.
5. Mix together the remaining seasonings and rub them all over the entire chicken.
6. Place the chicken back inside the inner pot, breast-side up, on top of the trivet and secure the lid to the sealing position. Press the Manual button and use the "+/-" button to set it for 25 minutes. When the timer beeps, allow the pressure to release naturally for 15 minutes. If the lid will not open at this point, quick release the remaining pressure and remove the chicken.
7. Let the chicken rest for 5 to 10 minutes before serving.

Nutritional Value: Calories 333; Fat 23g; Carbohydrates 9g; Protein 23g

Recipe 43: Garlic Honey Chicken

Serving Size: 5

Cooking Time: 6 hours

Ingredients:

- 10 chicken thighs
- 8.6 fl oz of soya sauce
- 8.9 fl oz of tomato ketchup
- 6.3 fl oz of honey
- 6 tsp of garlic
- 1 tsp of dried basil

Directions:

1. Add the chicken breasts to the slow cooker.
2. Mix ketchup, mustard, lemon juice, garlic granules, maple syrup, barbecue sauce, chili powder, cayenne pepper, and hot sauce in a mixing bowl until combined.
3. Pour the sauce over the chicken and cook for about 6 hours on low in the slow cooker.
4. Cook for another 30 minutes after shredding the chicken. Spoon the chicken and sauce into the sandwich rolls and serve.

Nutritional Value: Calories 255; Fat 3.1g; Carbohydrates 40.8g; Protein 19.6g

Recipe 44: Hawaiian Chicken Packets

Serving Size: 4

Cooking Time: 30 minutes

Ingredients:

- 4 skinless, chicken breast halves
- 1 green bell pepper, sliced
- 1 cup teriyaki sauce
- 1 onion, chopped
- 1 red bell pepper, sliced
- 20 oz. can pineapple chunks, drained

Directions:

1. Preheat the grill to medium-high. Place four squares of aluminum foil on the counter. In the center of each square, place one piece of chicken. Turn them over in the teriyaki sauce to coat them.
2. Distribute the red and green peppers, onion, and pineapple slices among the chicken pieces in equal numbers. Fold the foil in half and tuck it inside the packages. Cook for approximately about 20 minutes on the grill, or until the chicken is no longer pink and the juices flow clear.

Nutritional Value: Calories 304; Fat 1g; Carbohydrates 38g; Protein 33g

Recipe 45: Lamb and Pine Nut Aubergine

Serving Size: 4

Cooking Time: 25 minutes

Ingredients:

- 2 medium aubergines, cut into thick slices
- 5 tbsp olive oil, divided
- Sea salt
- Black pepper
- 1 small onion, minced
- 1 lb. ground lamb or pork
- 1 tbsp tomato paste
- 1 tsp garlic, minced
- ⅛ tsp ground allspice
- ½ cup plain yogurt
- ¼ cup pine nuts
- ¼ cup parsley, minced

Directions:

1. Preheat the oven to a heat of 375°F gas mark 5.
2. In a small heavy bottom pan on medium heat, add the pine nuts and toast until golden and fragrant. Set aside. Toss the aubergine slices in a large bowl with 4 tbsp of olive oil and spread them on a baking sheet. Season with prepared salt and pepper and bake for 25 minutes until lightly browned and soft.
3. In the meantime, in a large pan over medium-high heat, add the remaining 1 tbsp olive oil until hot. Add the onion and cook for 3 minutes until lightly browned.
4. Add the ground lamb or pork, breaking it up with a fork while it cooks for about 5 minutes, and add in the tomato paste. Cook for approximately about 2 minutes or until most of the acidity from the paste cooks down.
5. Mix the minced garlic and allspice into the meat mixture and season to taste. Cook for a further minute to incorporate.
6. Arrange the cooked aubergine slices on each plate and top it with the ground lamb or beef mixture. Drizzle with yogurt and sprinkle with toasted pine nuts and parsley.

Nutritional Value: Calories 625; Fat 60g; Carbohydrates 20g; Protein 24g

Recipe 46: Lamb Shanks with Burgundy Sauce

Serving Size: 4

Cooking Time: 8 hours

Ingredients:

- 4 lamb shanks
- 2 tbsp of parsley
- 2 tsp of garlic
- 1/2 tsp of oregano
- 1/2 tsp of lemon zest
- 2.6 oz of onion
- 1 Carrot
- 1 tsp of olive oil
- 8.8 fl oz of Burgundy wine
- 1 tsp of beef stock
- salt to taste
- pepper to taste

Directions:

1. Sauté the onion and carrot in oil in a small pot for about 3-4 minutes, or until soft. Combine the wine and beef stock. Bring the mixture to a boil, stirring regularly.
2. Put the lamb in a slow cooker. Season the lamb with salt and pepper and parsley, garlic, oregano, and lemon zest.
3. Pour over the mixture of the lamb. Cook on low for approximately about 8 hours, or until the meat is soft. Remove the lamb and keep it warm.
4. Bring juices to a boil in a small saucepan; simmer until liquid is reduced by half. Serve alongside lamb.

Nutritional Value: Calories 585; Fat 24g; Carbohydrates 18g; Protein 71g

Recipe 47: Lemon Pepper Tilapia with Broccoli and Carrots

Serving Size: 4

Cooking Time: 20 minutes

Ingredients:

- 1 pound (454 g) tilapia fillets
- 1 teaspoon lemon pepper seasoning
- ¼ teaspoon fine sea salt
- 2 tablespoons extra-virgin olive oil
- 2 garlic cloves, minced
- 1 small yellow onion, sliced
- ½ cup low-sodium vegetable broth
- 2 tablespoons fresh lemon juice
- 1 pound (454 g) broccoli crowns, cut into bite-size florets
- 8 ounces (227 g) carrots, cut into ¼-inch thick rounds

Directions:

1. Sprinkle the tilapia fillets all over with the lemon pepper seasoning and salt.
2. Select the Sauté setting on the Instant Pot and heat the oil and garlic for 2 minutes, until the garlic is bubbling but not browned. Add the onion and sauté for approximately about 3 minutes more, until it begins to soften.
3. Pour in the broth and lemon juice, then use a wooden spoon to nudge any browned bits from the bottom of the pot. Using tongs, add the fish fillets to the pot in a single layer; it's fine if they overlap slightly. Place the broccoli and carrots on top.
4. Secure the cover lid and set the Pressure Release to Sealing. Press the Cancel button to reset the cooking program, then select the Manual setting and set the cooking time for 1 minute at low pressure. (The pot will take about 10 minutes to come up to pressure before the cooking program begins.)
5. When the cooking program ends, let the pressure release naturally for 10 minutes (don't open the pot before the 10 minutes are up, even if the float valve has gone down), then move the Pressure Release to Venting to release any remaining steam. Open the pot. Use a fish spatula to transfer the vegetables and fillets to plates. Serve right away.

Nutritional Value: Calories 243; Fat 9g; Carbohydrates 15g; Protein 28g

Recipe 48: Lime Lamb Chops

Serving Size: 4

Cooking Time: 10 minutes

Ingredients:

- ¼ cup olive oil
- ¼ cup lime juice
- 2 tbsp lime zest
- 2 tbsp mint, chopped
- 2 tbsp parsley, chopped
- Pinch of Himalayan pink salt, ground
- Pinch black pepper, ground
- 12 lamb chops

Directions:

1. In a large-sized mixing bowl, whisk together the olive oil, lime juice, lime zest, chopped parsley, chopped mint, ground Himalayan pink salt, and ground black pepper.
2. Transfer the mixture into a marinading dish with a lid.
3. Add the lamb chops into the marinading dish and cover with the lid. Mix to combine.
4. Place the dish with the marinated lamb for 4 hours in the fridge, turning several times.
5. Preheat the oven to broil.
6. Remove the chops from the dish and arrange them on an aluminum foil-lined baking sheet. Discard the remaining marinade.
7. Broil the lamb chops for 4 minutes on each side.
8. Rest the lamb chops for approximately about 5 minutes before serving.

Nutritional Value: Calories 413; Fat 29g; Carbohydrates 10g; Protein 31g

Recipe 49: Lime Pulled Pork

Serving Size: 4

Cooking Time: 30 minutes

Ingredients:

- 1 tbsp. chili adobo sauce
- 1 tbsp. chili powder
- 2 tsp. salt
- 1 tsp. garlic powder
- 1 tsp. cumin
- 1/2 tsp. pepper
- 1 (2 1/2 to 3) pound cubed pork butt
- 1 tbsp. coconut oil
- 2 cups beef broth
- 1, cut into wedges lime
- 1/4 cup chopped cilantro

Directions:

1. In a bowl, mix pepper, cumin, garlic powder, salt, chili powder, and sauce.
2. Melt the oil on Sauté in the Instant Pot.
3. Rub the pork with spice mixture.
4. Place pork and sear for 3 to 5 minutes per side.
5. Add broth and close the lid.
6. Press Manual and cook 30 minutes.
7. Do a natural release and open.
8. Shred pork.
9. If you want crispy pork, then heat in a skillet until the pork is crisp.
10. Serve warm with cilantro garnish and fresh lime wedges.

Nutritional Value: Calories 570; Fat 35g; Carbohydrates 2g; Protein 55g

Recipe 50: Maple Pork with Figs

Serving Size: 4

Cooking Time: 25 minutes

Ingredients:

- 4 bone-in pork loin chops, ½ inch thick (about 1¼ lb), trimmed of fat
- ½ teaspoon salt
- ½ cup apple juice or dry red wine
- ¼ cup real maple syrup
- ⅓ cup coarsely chopped dried figs
- 1 teaspoon cornstarch
- ¼ cup water

Directions:

1. Spray 12-inch skillet with cooking spray; heat skillet over medium-high heat. Sprinkle pork with salt; place in skillet. Cook for approximately about 5 minutes, turning once, until browned. Remove from skillet; keep warm.
2. In same skillet, cook apple juice, maple syrup and figs over medium-high heat 5 minutes, stirring frequently.
3. In small bowl, mix cornstarch and water; stir into juice mixture. Cook over medium-high heat about 2 minutes, stirring constantly, until thickened and clear.
4. Reduce heat to medium. Return pork to skillet; spoon sauce over pork. Simmer about 2 minutes or until pork is no longer pink in center.

Nutritional Value: Calories 260; Fat 2.5g; Carbohydrates 26g; Protein 22g

Recipe 51: Pistachios and Herb Halibut

Serving Size: 4

Cooking Time: 20 minutes

Ingredients:

- 4 (5-oz) halibut fillets, lightly salted
- 2 tbsp olive oil, for coating
- ½ cup pistachios, unsalted and finely ground
- 1 tbsp parsley, finely chopped
- 1 tsp thyme, chopped
- 1 tsp basil, finely chopped
- Pinch of Himalayan pink salt, ground
- Black pepper, ground

Directions:

1. Warm the oven to 350°F gas mark 4. Cover the baking sheet with aluminum foil, set it aside.
2. Dry the halibut fillets with paper towels and place them on the baking sheet.
3. Coat the dried halibut fillets with olive oil.
4. In a small mixing bowl, add the finely ground pistachios, chopped parsley, chopped thyme, finely chopped basil, ground Himalayan pink salt, and ground black pepper, mix to combine.
5. Spoon the pistachio and herb mixture onto the halibut fish, spreading it out so the tops of the halibut fillets are covered.
6. Bake for 20 minutes until the halibut flakes when pressed with a fork
7. Serve warm.

Nutritional Value: Calories 262; Fat 11g; Carbohydrates 4g; Protein 32g

Recipe 52: Pork Chops with Apple Stuffing

Serving Size: 6

Cooking Time: 50 minutes

Ingredients:

- 1/4 cup chopped celery
- 1/4 cup chopped onion
- 1/4 cup sugar
- 1/4 tsp. pepper
- 1/4 tsp. salt
- 1/2 cup bread crumbs, or cracker crumbs
- 1 Tbsp. canola oil
- 2 tsp. chopped parsley
- 3 apples, peeled, cored, and diced
- 6 bone-in pork chops, at least 1-inch thick, and Approximately 2 lbs. total

Directions:

1. Chop a pocket approximately 1 1/2-inch deep into the side of each chop for stuffing.
2. Heat oil in frying pan.
3. Stir celery and onion into oil in frying pan. Cook over moderate until soft, stirring regularly.
4. Mix in diced apples. Drizzle with sugar.
5. Cover frying pan. Cook apples over low heat until soft and glazed.
6. Mix in bread crumbs.
7. Mix in salt, pepper, and parsley.
8. Spreading open the pocket in each chop with your fingers, stuff with mixture.
9. Place half of stuffed chops in frying pan. Brown on both sides over moderate to high heat.
10. Take out browned chops to platter. Cover to keep warm.
11. Repeat Step 9 with residual chops.
12. Return other chops to frying pan.
13. Reduce heat. Put in a few tablespoons of water.
14. Cover. Cook slowly over low heat until done, approximately 20-25 minutes.

Nutritional Value: Calories 270; Fat 9g; Carbohydrates 24g; Protein 24g

Recipe 53: Roast Chicken Casserole

Serving Size: 6

Cooking Time: 40 minutes

Ingredients:

- ½ cabbage, cut into chunks
- 1 red onion, chopped
- 1 white sweet potato, cut into chunks
- 6 tsp garlic, minced
- 2 tbsp olive oil, divided
- 2 tsp thyme, finely chopped
- Himalayan pink salt, ground
- Black pepper, ground
- 2½ lb. chicken quarters

Directions:

1. Preheat the oven to a heat of 450°F gas mark 8.
2. Lightly grease a large casserole dish and place the cabbage chunks, chopped onion, sweet potato chunks, and minced garlic in the dish. Add the 1 tbsp of olive oil, sprinkle with the chopped thyme, and season with ground Himalayan pink salt and ground black pepper.
3. Season the chicken to taste.
4. Using a heavy bottom large-sized pan on medium heat. Brown the chicken thighs and drumsticks in the remaining 1 tbsp of olive oil, for 10 minutes.
5. Place the browned chicken thighs and drumsticks on top of the vegetables in the casserole dish. Roast the chicken for about 30 minutes.

Nutritional Value: Calories 540; Fat 34g; Carbohydrates 14g; Protein 43g

Recipe 54: Roast Pork Tenderloin with Apple Slaw

Serving Size: 4

Cooking Time: 20 minutes

Ingredients:

- 2 tbsp avocado oil, divided
- 1 (1¼ lb.) pork tenderloin, boneless and patted dry
- Himalayan pink salt, ground
- Black pepper, ground
- 1 tbsp rosemary, chopped
- 1 Granny Smith apple, cored, seeded cut into wedges
- ½ red cabbage, thinly sliced and core removed
- ½ red onion, thinly sliced
- 1 tbsp apple cider vinegar
- ½ cup parsley, roughly chopped
- 1 tbsp mint, chopped

Directions:

1. Preheat the oven to 425°F gas mark 7.
2. Heat 1 tbsp avocado oil in a large cast-iron pan over medium heat until hot.
3. Rub the dried pork generously with ground Himalayan pink salt, ground black pepper, and the finely chopped rosemary.
4. Transfer the pork into the pan, and sear for about 10 minutes, until browned on all sides.
5. In a prepared large-sized mixing bowl, add the apple wedges, sliced cabbage, and sliced onion with the remaining 1 tbsp of avocado oil. Scatter the mixture around the pork in the cast iron pan.
6. Place the large-sized pan into the oven, and roast for 10 minutes, until the pork is fully cooked, and the vegetables are tender.
7. Put the cooked pork onto a cutting board and allow to rest.
8. Add the apple cider vinegar, chopped mint, and chopped parsley into the pan with the apple wedges and cabbage and mix well.
9. Slice the already cooked pork and serve with the slaw.

Nutritional Value: Calories 263; Fat 11g; Carbohydrates 15g; Protein 28g

Recipe 55: Salisbury Steak in Mushroom Sauce

Serving Size: 4

Cooking Time: 15 minutes

Ingredients:

- 1 pound 85% lean ground beef
- 1 tsp. Steak seasoning
- 1 Egg
- 2 Tbsp. Butter
- 1/2, sliced Onion
- 1/2 cup Sliced button mushrooms
- 1 cup Beef broth
- 2 oz. Cream cheese
- 1/4 cup Heavy cream
- 1/4 tsp. Xanthan gum

Directions:

2. Mix egg, steak seasoning, and ground beef in a bowl. Make 4 patties and set aside.
3. Press Sauté and melt the butter.
4. Add mushrooms and onion and stir-fry for 3 to 5 minutes.
5. Press Cancel and add beef patties, broth, and cream cheese to the Instant Pot.
6. Close the lid and press Manual.
7. Cook 15 minutes on High.
8. Do a natural release when done.
9. Remove the patties and set aside.
10. Add xanthan gum and heavy cream. Whisk to mix.
11. Reduce the sauce on Sauté for 5 to 10 minutes.
12. Press Cancel and add patties back to the Instant Pot.
13. Serve.

Nutritional Value: Calories 420; Fat 30g; Carbohydrates 2g; Protein 25g

Recipe 56: Sausage Pasta

Serving Size: 2

Cooking Time: 35 minutes

Ingredients:

- 1 tbsp of olive oil
- 8 oz of turkey sausage
- 1 red bell pepper
- 1/2 cup of onion
- 4 cups of kale
- 2 garlic cloves
- 1/4 tsp of red pepper
- 2 cups of water
- 3/4 cup of penne pasta
- 2 tbsp of cheese

Directions:

1. In a large-sized saucepan, heat the oil over medium-high heat. Cook, occasionally tossing until the sausage is no longer pink. Place on a plate to cool. Cook occasionally turns until the bell pepper and onion are softened, about 5 minutes.
2. Stir in the kale, garlic, red pepper, and sausage. Cook, constantly stirring, until the kale is wilted. Bring to a boil, occasionally stirring, after adding the water and pasta. Reduce the heat to medium, cover, and cook for about 10 minutes until the pasta is soft.
3. Serve immediately with a sprinkling of Parmesan cheese.

Nutritional Value: Calories 463; Fat 19g; Carbohydrates 46.3g; Protein 30g

Recipe 57: Sesame Chicken with Couscous

Serving Size: 4

Cooking Time: 15 minutes

Ingredients:

- 1½ cups water
- 1 tbsp. olive oil
- 1 cup whole wheat couscous, uncooked
- 4 green onions, sliced
- 2 cups coleslaw mix
- 2 cups cooked chicken breast, shredded
- 2 tbsp. + ½ cup low-fat sesame salad dressing, divided
- Chopped peanuts, optional
- 2 tbsp. fresh cilantro, minced

Directions:

1. Bring water to a very hot boil in a small saucepan. Toss in the couscous. Remove from heat and let aside for 5-10 minutes, covered, until water has been absorbed. Using a fork, fluff the mixture. Heat the oil in a large nonstick skillet over medium heat. Cook and stir for 3-4 minutes, or just until the coleslaw mix is tender.
2. Mix and cook the green onions, 2 tbsp. dressing, and couscous. Remove couscous from pan and set aside to keep warm. Add the chicken and the remaining 1/2 cup dressing to the same skillet and cook and mix over medium heat until cooked through. Serve over couscous with cilantro and peanuts, if preferred.

Nutritional Value: Calories 320; Fat 9g; Carbohydrates 35g; Protein 26g

Recipe 58: Sweet and Tangy Salmon

Serving Size: 4

Cooking Time: 20 minutes

Ingredients:

- 4 salmon fillets
- 2 tbsp. brown sugar
- 1 tbsp. butter
- 2 tbsp. Dijon mustard
- 2 tbsp. low-sodium soy sauce
- ½ tsp. pepper
- 1/8 tsp. salt
- 1 tbsp. olive oil
- 1 lb. fresh green beans, trimmed

Directions:

1. Preheat the oven to 425°F. Fill a 15x10-inch baking pan with fillets and spray with cooking spray. Melt butter in a large-sized pan, and then add soy sauce, brown sugar, oil, mustard, pepper, and salt. Half of the sauce should be brushed over the fish.
2. Toss green beans in a large mixing dish with the remaining brown sugar sauce to coat. Arrange the prepared green beans in a circle around the fillets. Roast for 14-16 minutes, or until green beans are crisp-tender and fish flakes easily with a fork.

Nutritional Value: Calories 394; Fat 22g; Carbohydrates 17g; Protein 31g

Recipe 59: Thyme Turkey Breast

Serving Size: 4

Cooking Time: 40 minutes

Ingredients:

- 2 lb. turkey breast
- Salt, to taste
- Black pepper, to taste
- 4 tablespoon butters, melted
- 3 cloves garlic, minced
- 1 teaspoon thyme, chopped
- 1 teaspoon rosemary, chopped

Directions:

1. Mix butter with salt, black pepper, garlic, thyme, and rosemary in a bowl.
2. Rub this seasoning over the turkey breast liberally and place it in the Air Fryer basket.
3. Turn the dial to actually select the "Air Fry" mode.
4. Hit the Time button and again use the dial to set the cooking time to 40 minutes
5. Now push the Temp button and rotate the dial to set the temperature at 375 °F.
6. Once preheated, place the Air fryer basket inside the oven
7. Slice and serve fresh.

Nutritional Value: Calories 334; Fat 5g; Carbohydrates 54g; Protein 26g

Recipe 60: Walnut and Oat-Crusted Cod

Serving Size: 4

Cooking Time: 15 minutes

Ingredients:

- 2 Cod fillets (6 ounces each), skin removed
- 1/4 teaspoon salt
- 1/4 teaspoon pepper
- 3 tablespoons quick-cooking oats, crushed
- 3 tablespoons finely chopped pecans
- 2 tablespoons olive oil

Directions:

1. Preheat the oven to 400 °. Place the cod on the baking sheet.
2. Sprinkle with salt and pepper. Mix the remaining ingredients; Squeeze the cod.
3. Bake for approximately about 12 to 15 minutes until the fish flakes easily with a fork.

Nutritional Value: Calories 494; Fat 33.4g; Carbohydrates 6.5g; Protein 44.9g

Chapter 3: Dinner Recipes

Recipe 61: Artichoke Ratatouille Chicken

Serving Size: 6

Cooking Time: 1 hour

Ingredients:

- 1 lb. Japanese eggplants
- 1 sweet yellow pepper
- 4 plum tomatoes
- 1 medium onion
- 1 sweet red pepper
- 2 tbsp. minced fresh thyme
- 14 oz. artichoke hearts, drained and quartered
- 2 tbsp. olive oil
- 2 tbsp. capers, drained
- 1 tsp. Creole seasoning, divided
- 2 garlic cloves, minced
- 1 cup white wine
- 1½ lb. skinless chicken breasts, cubed
- ¼ cup grated Asiago cheese

Directions:

1. Transfer tomatoes, eggplants, onion and peppers to a large mixing bowl and cut into 3/4-inch pieces. Add 1/2 tsp. Creole seasoning, artichoke hearts, capers, thyme, oil, garlic Season the chicken with the rest of the Creole spice.
2. Place the prepared chicken in a 13x9-inch baking dish covered with cooking spray, and top with the vegetable mixture. Pour wine over the veggies. Preheat oven to a heat of 350°F and bake for 30 minutes, covered. Uncover and bake for another 30-45 minutes, or until the chicken is no longer pink and the veggies are soft. Cheese should be sprinkled on top.

Nutritional Value: Calories 252; Fat 9g; Carbohydrates 15g; Protein 28g

Recipe 62: Baked Turkey Spaghetti

Serving Size: 4

Cooking Time: 20 minutes

Ingredients:

- 1 (10-ounce / 283-g) package zucchini noodles
- 2 tablespoons extra-virgin olive oil, divided
- 1 pound (454 g) 93% lean ground turkey
- 1/2 teaspoon dried oregano
- 2 cups low-sodium spaghetti sauce
- 1/2 cup shredded sharp Cheddar cheese

Directions:

1. Pat the prepared zucchini noodles dry between two paper towels.
2. In an oven-safe medium skillet, heat 1 tablespoon of olive oil over medium heat. When hot, add the zucchini noodles. Cook for 3 minutes, stirring halfway through.
3. Add the remaining 1 tablespoon of oil, ground turkey, and oregano. Cook for 7 to 10 minutes, stirring and breaking apart, as needed.
4. Add the spaghetti sauce to the skillet and stir.
5. If your broiler is in the top of your oven, place the oven rack in the center position. Set the broiler on high.
6. Top the mixture with the cheese, and broil for 5 minutes or until the cheese is bubbly.

Nutritional Value: Calories 335; Fat 21g; Carbohydrates 12g; Protein 28g

Recipe 63: Basil Grilled Shrimp

Serving Size: 6

Cooking Time: 10 minutes

Ingredients:

- 1 tbsp. olive oil
- 1 lb. medium fresh shrimp
- ½ lemon juice
- 1 tbsp. coarse-grain prepared mustard
- 1½ tbsp. reduced-calorie margarine, melted
- 1 clove garlic, minced
- 1 cup fresh basil, minced
- pinch of black pepper
- Cooking spray

Directions:

1. Whisk together margarine, olive oil, mustard, lemon juice, garlic, basil, and pepper in a small bowl; transfer to a large zip-top bag. Toss in the shrimp and gently toss to coat. Refrigerate for 1 hour to marinate. Heat the grill to medium-high. Remove the shrimp from the sauce and skewer them. Spray the grill grate with nonstick cooking spray.
2. Place the skewers on the grill over medium high heat and sprinkle with any leftover marinade. Cook for approximatey about 2–3 minutes, then flip the shrimp and cook for another 2–3 minutes, or until pink and opaque.

Nutritional Value: Calories 180; Fat 8g; Carbohydrates 3g; Protein 24g

Recipe 64: Cajun Coconut Cream Prawns

Serving Size: 3

Cooking Time: 10 minutes

Ingredients:

- 2 tsp coconut oil
- ½ red onion, finely chopped
- 1 tbsp Cajun seasoning, shop-bought
- 1 lb. large prawn tails, deshelled and deveined
- ¼ cup coconut cream
- 1 tbsp parsley, finely chopped (optional)

Directions:

1. Heat the prepared coconut oil in a large heavy bottom pan over medium-high heat until hot. Fry the finely chopped onion for 3 minutes until soft.
2. Add the Cajun seasoning and fry for 1 minute.
3. Mix in the prawns and fry for 6 minutes until fully cooked and pink, stirring occasionally. Add the prepared coconut cream and stir to incorporate.
4. Garnish with parsley (if using) and serve.

Nutritional Value: Calories 200; Fat 8g; Carbohydrates 6g; Protein 31g

Recipe 65: Chicken and Apricot Tagine

Serving Size: 4

Cooking Time: 35 minutes

Ingredients:

- 675g boneless chicken chunks
- 1 medium onion, finely chopped
- 1 tsp. ground ginger
- 1 tbsp. olive oil
- 1 tsp. ground coriander
- 1 tsp. cinnamon
- 1 tsp. ground cumin
- 1 tsp. turmeric
- 1 tbsp. tomato puree
- pinch of chilli powder
- 150g dried apricots
- 1 small orange, zested and juiced
- 2 cups chicken stock
- 2 tbsp. fresh coriander, chopped

Directions:

1. In a large-sized casserole pot, heat the oil over low heat. Add onions and cook until the onion is tender, then add the ground spices. Stir in the chicken and tomato puree to cover all of the pieces with the spice mixture.
2. After that, add orange juice and zest, chicken stock and dried apricots. Bring to a very hot boil, then lower to a low heat and cover the pan, letting it to gently simmer for 30 minutes, or until the chicken is cooked and the fluids run clear, the sauce has slightly reduced, and the fruits are soft and plump.
3. Season the Tangine to taste with salt and pepper. Before serving, stir in the chopped coriander.

Nutritional Value: Calories 343; Fat 12g; Carbohydrates 31g; Protein 39g

Recipe 66: Chicken Fajitas

Serving Size: 4

Cooking Time: 20 minutes

Ingredients:

- 2 tbsp. extra-virgin olive oil
- 1 lb. boneless, skinless chicken breasts
- 2 tsp. ground cumin
- 1 tbsp. chili powder
- ¾ tsp. salt
- 1 tsp. garlic powder
- 1 large yellow bell pepper, sliced
- 1 large red bell pepper, sliced
- 1 tbsp. lime juice
- 1 large onion, sliced

Directions:

1. Preheat the oven to 400°F. Using cooking spray, coat a large, rimmed baking sheet. Chicken breasts should be cut in half horizontally, then crosswise into strips.
2. In a large mixing bowl, combine the oil, chili powder, garlic powder, cumin, and salt. Stir in the chicken to coat it in the spice mixture. Stir in the bell peppers and onion until everything is well combined. Spread the chicken and veggies in an equal layer on the prepared baking sheet.
3. Roast for 15 minutes on the center rack. Turn the broiler to high and leave the pan in place. Broil for another 5 minutes or until the chicken is cooked properly and the veggies are browning in places. Remove the dish from the oven. Add the lime juice and mix well.

Nutritional Value: Calories 356; Fat 12g; Carbohydrates 32g; Protein 30g

Recipe 67: Chicken with Bell Pepper Thyme Sauce

Serving Size: 4

Cooking Time: 30 minutes

Ingredients:

- 4 (4 oz) chicken breasts, deboned and skinless
- Himalayan pink salt, ground
- Black pepper, ground
- 1 tbsp olive oil
- ½ red onion, finely chopped
- ½ medium red, green, and yellow bell pepper, sliced
- 1 cup chicken broth, low in salt
- 2 tsp thyme, chopped
- ¼ cup coconut cream
- 1 tbsp plant-based butter
- 1 spring onion, chopped

Directions:

1. Preheat the oven to a heat of 375°F gas mark 5.
2. Season the chicken breasts with ground Himalayan pink salt and ground black pepper.
3. In a large ovenproof frying pan on medium-high heat, add the olive oil and cook until hot.
4. Lightly brown the chicken breasts for 5 minutes on each side. Place the chicken breasts onto a rimmed plate to rest.
5. In the same pan, fry the finely chopped onion until translucent, add the sliced red, green and yellow peppers and fry for 3 minutes until softened.
6. Pour in the chicken broth and chopped thyme. Simmer for 6 minutes until the liquid has reduced by half.
7. Mix in the coconut cream and the plant-based butter and return the chicken breasts and any accumulated juices on the plate into the pan. Allow thickening.
8. Place the ovenproof pan into the oven and bake for 10 minutes until cooked through.
9. Serve hot with the chopped spring onion.

Nutritional Value: Calories 287; Fat 14g; Carbohydrates 4g; Protein 34g

Recipe 68: Chili Pork Tenderloin

Serving Size: 3

Cooking Time: 35 minutes

Ingredients:

- 1 tablespoon lime juice
- 1 teaspoon chili powder
- 1 teaspoon reduced-sodium soy sauce
- 1/2 teaspoon sugar
- 1/2 teaspoon salt
- 1/4 teaspoon pepper
- 1 pork tenderloin (1 pound)
- 1 tablespoon canola oil

Directions:

1. In a large-sized bowl, combine the first six ingredients; brush over pork.
2. In a large ovenproof skillet, brown pork in oil on all sides.
3. Bake at 375° for 25-30 minutes or until a thermometer reads 145°.
4. Let stand for 5 minutes before slicing.

Nutritional Value: Calories 224; Fat 10g; Carbohydrates 2g; Protein 30g

Recipe 69: Cinnamon Chicken

Serving Size: 4

Cooking Time: 30 minutes

Ingredients:

- 4 skinless, chicken breast halves
- 2 tbsp. Italian-style seasoning
- 1 tsp. ground cinnamon
- 3 tsp. salt
- 1½ tsp. garlic powder
- 1 tsp. ground black pepper

Directions:

1. Preheat the oven to 350°F.
2. Place the chicken in a 9x13 inch baking dish that has been lightly oiled.
3. Season with seasoning, ground cinnamon, salt, garlic powder, and pepper, and mix well.
4. Bake for 30 minutes at 350°F or until chicken is baked through and juices flow clear.

Nutritional Value: Calories 143; Fat 1g; Carbohydrates 3g; Protein 27g

Recipe 70: Crusted Red Snapper

Serving Size: 4

Cooking Time: 15 minutes

Ingredients:

- 1 lb. red snapper fillets
- ¼ cup grated parmesan cheese
- 1/3 cup Panko breadcrumbs
- Salt and pepper to taste
- 3 tbsp. olive oil
- 2 tbsp. fat-free mayonnaise
- ½ tsp. garlic powder

Directions:

1. Preheat the oven to 450 degrees.
2. Combine all ingredients except the red snapper and the olive oil.
3. Coat the fish with the mixture and transfer to a baking dish.
4. Drizzle the fish with the olive oil.
5. Bake for 14 minutes. The fish should be flaky.

Nutritional Value: Calories 215; Fat 7.9g; Carbohydrates 8g; Protein 28.2g

Recipe 71: Curry Turkey Stir-Fry

Serving Size: 4

Cooking Time: 10 minutes

Ingredients:

- ½ tsp. cornstarch
- 1 tbsp. fresh cilantro, minced
- 2 tbsp. low-sodium soy sauce
- 1 tsp. curry powder
- 1 garlic clove, minced
- 1 tbsp. honey
- 1 tsp. sesame oil
- 1/8 tsp. crushed red pepper flakes
- 1 sweet red pepper, julienned
- 3 green onions
- 2 cups cooked turkey breast, cubed
- 1 tbsp. canola oil
- 2 cups cooked brown rice

Directions:

1. Combine the first eight ingredients and make a sauce. Heat canola oil in a large pan over medium-high heat and stir-fry red pepper for 2 minutes, until crisp-tender. Stir in green onions and cook for 1-2 minutes, or until tender. Add the cornstarch sauce to the pan and stir well. Bring to a very hot boil, then simmer and stir for 1-2 minutes, or until the sauce has thickened. Heat thoroughly the turkey by stirring it in. Serve with a side of rice.

Nutritional Value: Calories 287; Fat 7g; Carbohydrates 31g; Protein 25g

Recipe 72: Ginger Cod Chard Bake

Serving Size: 4

Cooking Time: 15 minutes

Ingredients:

- 1 chard bunch, stemmed, leaves and stems cut into thin strips
- 1 red bell pepper, strips
- 1 pound (454 g) cod fillets cut into 4 pieces
- 1 tablespoon grated fresh ginger
- 3 garlic cloves, minced
- 2 tablespoons white wine vinegar
- 2 tablespoons low-sodium tamari or gluten-free soy sauce
- ½ tablespoon honey

Directions:

2. Preheat the oven to a heat of 425°F (220°C).
3. Cut four pieces of prepared parchment paper, each about 16 inches wide. Lay the four pieces out on a large workspace.
4. On each piece of paper, arrange a small pile of chard leaves and stems, topped by several strips of bell pepper. Top with a piece of cod.
5. In a large-sized bowl, mix the ginger, garlic, vinegar, tamari, and honey. Top each piece of prepared fish with one-fourth of the mixture.
6. Fold the parchment paper over so the edges overlap. Fold the edges over several times to secure the fish in the packets. Carefully place the packets on a large baking sheet.
7. Bake for 12 minutes. Carefully open the packets, allowing steam to escape, and serve.

Nutritional Value: Calories 120; Fat 1g; Carbohydrates 8.9g; Protein 19.1g

Recipe 73: Halibut Ceviche with Cilantro

Serving Size: 4

Cooking Time: 0 minutes

Ingredients:

- ½ pound (227 g) fresh skinless, white, ocean fish fillet (halibut, mahi mahi, etc.), diced
- 1 cup freshly squeezed lime juice, divided
- 2 tablespoons chopped fresh cilantro, divided
- 1 Serrano pepper, sliced
- 1 garlic clove, crushed
- ¾ teaspoon salt, divided
- ½ red onion, thinly sliced
- 2 tomatoes, diced
- 1 red bell pepper, seeded and diced
- 1 tablespoon extra-virgin olive oil

Directions:

1. In a large-sized mixing bowl, combine the fish, ¾ cup of lime juice, 1 tablespoon of cilantro, Serrano pepper, garlic, and ½ teaspoon of salt.
2. The fish should be covered or nearly covered in lime juice. Cover the large-sized bowl and refrigerate for 4 hours.
3. Sprinkle the remaining ¼ teaspoon of salt over the onion in a small bowl, and let sit for 10 minutes. Drain and rinse well.
4. In a large-sized bowl, combine the tomatoes, bell pepper, olive oil, remaining ¼ cup of lime juice, and onion. Let rest for approximately about at least 10 minutes, or as long as 4 hours, while the fish "cooks."
5. When the fish is actually ready, it will be completely white and opaque. At this time, strain the juice, reserving it in another bowl. If desired, remove the Serrano pepper and garlic.
6. Add the vegetables to the fish, and stir gently. Taste, and add some of the reserved lime juice to the ceviche as desired. Serve topped with the remaining 1 tablespoon of cilantro.

Nutritional Value: Calories 122; Fat 4.1g; Carbohydrates 11.1g; Protein 11.9g

Recipe 74: Herb-Grilled Bass

Serving Size: 4

Cooking Time: 20 minutes

Ingredients:

- 2 bass fillets
- ½ tsp. onion powder
- ½ tsp. garlic salt
- ¼ tsp. lemon pepper
- ½ tsp. paprika
- ½ clove minced garlic
- 1 tbsp. reduced-calorie margarine
- ¼ tsp. dried parsley
- Cooking spray

Directions:

1. Preheat the grill to medium. Using olive oil cooking spray, lightly coat both sides of the fish fillets. In a small bowl, combine the onion powder, garlic salt, lemon pepper and paprika and whisk well to combine.
2. Season both sides of the prepared fish fillets with the seasoning mixture. Heat the margarine, garlic, with parsley in a skillet over medium heat just before grilling.
3. When the margarine has actually melted, remove from the heat and cover to keep warm. Cooking spray the grill rack or grill basket. 4–6 minutes per side on the grill, or until salmon flakes easily with a fork. Drizzle the margarine mixture over the fish.

Nutritional Value: Calories 133; Fat 5g; Carbohydrates 1g; Protein 21g

Recipe 75: Lime and Orange Grilled Scallops

Serving Size: 4

Cooking Time: 10 minutes

Ingredients:

- 2 lb. scallops, cleaned and dried
- Himalayan pink salt
- Black pepper, ground
- 2 tbsp olive oil
- 1 tbsp garlic, minced
- ¼ cup fresh orange juice
- 1 tsp orange zest
- 2 limes, juiced and zested
- 2 tsp thyme, chopped for garnish

Directions:

1. Season the clean and dried scallops with ground Himalayan pink salt and ground black pepper.
2. Over medium heat, add the prepared olive oil into a grill pan until hot.
3. Fry the minced garlic for 3 minutes until softened.
4. Gently place the scallops into the pan and cook for 4 minutes on each side, until lightly seared.
5. Place the grilled scallops onto a plate and cover. Set aside.
6. Add the fresh orange juice, orange zest, lime juice, and lime zest into the pan and stir scraping up the bottom bits.
7. Drizzle the orange and lime sauce over the scallops and garnish with chopped thyme and serve.

Nutritional Value: Calories 267; Fat 8g; Carbohydrates 8g; Protein 38g

Recipe 76: Mussels in Tomato Sauce

Serving Size: 4

Cooking Time: 30 minutes

Ingredients:

- 2 tomatoes, seeded and chopped finely
- 2 pounds mussels, scrubbed and de-bearded
- 1 cup low-sodium chicken broth
- 1 tablespoon fresh lemon juice
- 2 garlic cloves, minced

Directions:

1. In the pot of Instant Pot, place tomatoes, garlic, wine and bay leaf and stir to combine.
2. Arrange the mussels on top.
3. Close the cover lid and place the pressure valve to "Seal" position.
4. Press "Manual" and cook under "High Pressure" for about 3 minutes.
5. Press "Cancel" and carefully allow a "Quick" release.
6. Open the lid and serve hot.

Nutritional Value: Calories 213; Fat 25.2g; Carbohydrates 11g; Protein 28.2g

Recipe 77: Orange Tilapia

Serving Size: 4

Cooking Time: 10 minutes

Ingredients:

- 2 tbsp. olive oil
- 4 tilapia fillets
- ½ tsp. Old Bay seasoning
- Salt and pepper to taste
- ½ tsp. lemon basil
- 5 tbsp. juice from a fresh orange
- 3 tbsp. juice from a fresh lemon

Directions:

1. Heat the oil in a skillet.
2. Season the tilapia with Old Bay seasoning, salt, pepper, and lemon basil.
3. Top with the orange and lemon juices.
4. Cook for 8 minutes. The fish should be flaky.

Nutritional Value: Calories 135.7; Fat 3.9g; Carbohydrates 8g; Protein 18.1g

Recipe 78: Peppery Halibut Fillet with Beans

Serving Size: 4

Cooking Time: 15 minutes

Ingredients:

- 1 pound (454 g) green beans, trimmed
- 2 red bell peppers, strips
- 1 onion, sliced
- Zest and juice of 2 lemons
- 3 garlic cloves, minced
- 2 tablespoons extra-virgin olive oil
- 1 teaspoon dried dill
- 1 teaspoon dried oregano
- 4 (4-ounce / 113-g) halibut fillets
- ½ teaspoon salt
- ¼ teaspoons freshly ground black pepper

Directions:

1. Preheat the oven to a heat of 400°F (205°C). Line a baking sheet with parchment paper.
2. In a large bowl, toss the green beans, bell peppers, onion, lemon zest and juice, garlic, olive oil, dill, and oregano.
3. Use a slotted spoon to transfer the vegetables to the prepared baking sheet in a single layer, leaving the juice behind in the bowl.
4. Gently place the halibut fillets in the bowl, and coat in the juice.
5. Transfer the fillets to the baking sheet, nestled between the vegetables, and drizzle them with any juice left in the bowl.
6. Sprinkle the vegetables and halibut with the salt and pepper.
7. Bake for 15 to 20 minutes until the vegetables are just tender and the fish flakes apart easily.

Nutritional Value: Calories 235; Fat 9.1g; Carbohydrates 16.1g; Protein 23.9g

Recipe 79: Ricotta and Turkey Bell Peppers

Serving Size: 4

Cooking Time: 50 minutes

Ingredients:

- Non-stick cooking spray
- 1 tsp olive oil
- 1 lb. turkey breast, ground
- ½ red onion, finely chopped
- 1 tsp garlic, crushed
- 1 tomato, finely chopped
- 2 medium carrots, cubes
- ¼ cup peas, thawed
- ½ tsp basil, finely chopped
- Himalayan pink salt
- Black pepper, ground
- 4 medium red bell peppers, seeds removed
- 2 oz ricotta cheese, crumbled
- ¼ cup water

Directions:

1. Heat the oven to 350°F or gas mark 4. Use non-stick cooking spray to coat a baking dish and set it aside.
2. In a heavy bottom pan, heat the 1 tsp olive oil until hot. Add the ground turkey into the pan and cook for 6 minutes using a fork to break up the ground turkey until it is browned.
3. Add and fry the finely chopped onion, cubed carrots, thawed peas, and crushed garlic for 3 minutes until softened. Stir in the finely chopped tomato and chopped basil. Season with ground Himalayan pink salt and ground black pepper.
4. Place the red bell peppers cut side up in the baking dish. Spoon the filling equally into the 4 bell pepper. Sprinkle the crumbled ricotta cheese on top of the filling.
5. Gently add ¼ cup of water into the baking dish and cover with aluminum foil.
6. Bake for 40 minutes until the peppers are soft.

Nutritional Value: Calories 280; Fat 14g; Carbohydrates 9g; Protein 24g

Recipe 80: Roasted Beef with Shallot Sauce

Serving Size: 4

Cooking Time: 1 hour 40 minutes

Ingredients:

- 1 ½ lb (680 g) top rump beef roast
- Salt and pepper to taste
- 3 teaspoons extra-virgin olive oil, divided
- 3 shallots, minced
- 2 teaspoons minced garlic
- 1 tablespoon green peppercorns
- 2 tablespoons dry sherry
- 2 tablespoons all-purpose flour
- 1 cup sodium-free beef broth

Directions:

1. Preheat the oven to 300°F.
2. Season the roast with salt and pepper.
3. Place a large-sized skillet over medium-high heat and add 2 teaspoons of olive oil.
4. Brown the beef on all sides and transfer the roast to a baking dish.
5. Roast until desired doneness, about 1½ hours for medium. Roast in the oven for 1 hour and start the sauce.
6. In a large-sized saucepan over medium-high heat, sauté the shallots in the remaining 1 teaspoon of olive oil until translucent, about 4 minutes.
7. Stir in the garlic and peppercorns, and cook for another minute. Whisk in the sherry to deglaze the pan.
8. Whisk in the flour to thicken, cooking for 1 minute and stirring constantly.
9. Pour in the broth and whisk until the sauce is thick and glossy, about 4 minutes. Season the sauce with salt and pepper.
10. Serve the beef with a generous spoonful of sauce.

Nutritional Value: Calories 331; Fat 18g; Carbohydrates 2g; Protein 36.1g

Recipe 81: Roasted Sea Bass

Serving Size: 6

Cooking Time: 15 minutes

Ingredients:

- ¼ cup olive oil
- 6 sea bass filets
- Fine-grained kosher salt and freshly ground black pepper to taste
- ¼ cup dry white wine
- 3 teaspoons fresh dill
- 2 teaspoons fresh thyme
- 1 garlic clove, minced

Directions:

1. Preheat the oven to 425°F.
2. Grease the roasting pan with olive oil.
3. Put the fish in a pan and grease it with oil.
4. Season with salt and pepper.
5. Add the ingredients and pour over the fish. Bake for 10-15 minutes.
6. sea bass is done when the flesh is firm and opaque.

Nutritional Value: Calories 213; Fat 12g; Carbohydrates 3g; Protein 24g

Recipe 82: Roasted Tilapia and Tomatoes with Garlic

Serving Size: 4

Cooking Time: 15 minutes

Ingredients:

- 1-pint cherry tomatoes, halved
- 2 tablespoons coconut oil, divided
- 2 teaspoons garlic powder
- 1 tablespoon chopped fresh thyme
- ½ teaspoon salt, divided
- ½ teaspoon ground pepper, divided
- 1 ¼ pounds Tilapia fillet, cut into 4 portions

Directions:

1. Preheat the oven to 400 degrees F.
2. Combine tomatoes, 1 tbsp. oil, garlic powder, thyme, 1/4 teaspoon salt and 1/4 teaspoon pepper in a medium bowl. Distribute the mixture in the center of a large tray mounted on the rim. Spread the remaining 1 tablespoon of oil over the pieces of Tilapia. Sprinkle with the remaining quarter teaspoon of salt and pepper. Place on the empty side of the baking sheet. Bake, 12 to 15 minutes, until the tomatoes are broken and the salmon is cooked through. Pour the tomato mixture over the Tilapia.

Nutritional Value: Calories 150; Fat 10.1g; Carbohydrates 5.1g; Protein 11.4g

Recipe 83: Rosemary Chicken

Serving Size: 2

Cooking Time: 30 minutes

Ingredients:

- 2 tsp. olive oil
- 1 tbsp. fresh lemon juice
- 1 clove garlic, minced
- 1 tsp. lemon zest
- 1/8 tsp. salt
- 1 tbsp. fresh rosemary, chopped
- 2 chicken breast halves, skinless
- 1/8 tsp. pepper
- nonstick cooking spray
- 1 tbsp. balsamic vinegar
- 3 tbsp. low-sodium barbeque sauce
- 1 tsp. honey

Directions:

1. Combine the oil, lemon juice, lemon zest, garlic, salt, rosemary, and pepper in a nonmetallic bowl. Toss in the chicken and flip to coat. Refrigerate for 30 minutes, covered. Using cooking spray, lightly coat the grill rack.
2. Preheat the grill to medium-high temperature. Grill the marinated chicken for approximately about 4 to 5 minutes per side, or until the middle is no longer pink.
3. Meanwhile, combine the vinegar, barbecue sauce, and honey in a small pot. Cook the sauce stirring periodically, for 3 to 4 minutes over medium-low heat, or until well cooked. Pour the sauce over the chicken that has been cooked.

Nutritional Value: Calories 235; Fat 7g; Carbohydrates 17g; Protein 24g

Recipe 84: Salmon Fish Cakes

Serving Size: 4

Cooking Time: 30 minutes

Ingredients:

- 3 potatoes, diced
- Salt and pepper, to taste
- 1 cup cooked salmon
- 2 tbsp. fresh grated parmesan
- 1 tbsp. olive oil
- 1 bunch parsley, chopped
- 4 tbsp. flour
- 1 cup breadcrumbs
- 1 egg, lightly beaten

Directions:

1. Peel the prepared potatoes and boil them until they are cooked, then drain and mash. Combine the potatoes, salmon, a pinch of salt and pepper, and half of the parsley in a mixing bowl. Form into round cakes with a mold.
2. Combine the breadcrumbs, parmesan, and the remaining parsley in a mixing bowl.
3. Before rolling the fish cakes in the breadcrumb mixture, coat them in flour and then in beaten egg. In a frying pan, heat the olive oil and gently cook the fish cakes for 4 minutes on each side, or until golden brown. Before serving, remove from the pan and lay on absorbent paper.

Nutritional Value: Calories 234; Fat 4g; Carbohydrates 6g; Protein 10g

Recipe 85: Salmon in Ginger Cream

Serving Size: 4

Cooking Time: 15 minutes

Ingredients:

- 2 tablespoons (28 g) butter
- 2 pieces salmon fillet, 6 ounces (170 g) each, skin still attached
- 1 teaspoon minced garlic or 2 cloves garlic, crushed
- 2 scallions, finely minced
- 2 tablespoons (2 g) chopped cilantro
- 4 tablespoons (60 ml) dry white wine
- 2 tablespoons (16 g) grated gingerroot
- 4 tablespoons (60 g) sour cream
- Salt and pepper

Directions:

1. Melt the prepared butter in a cooking pan over medium-low heat and start cooking the salmon. Fry them for 4 minutes on each side.
2. When the fish is fried, crush the garlic, mince the green onions and mince the cilantro.
3. When the salmon has cooked on both sides for 4 minutes, add the wine to the pot and then replace the lid. Cook for approximately about another 2 minutes, until the fish is cooked through.
4. Transfer the fish to a plate.
5. Add the garlic, green onions, cilantro, and ginger to the wine and butter in a skillet to medium-high and cook for 1-2 minutes.
6. Add sour cream, mix and season with salt and pepper.
7. Serve with sauce.

Nutritional Value: Calories 265; Fat 5g; Carbohydrates 4g; Protein 36g

Recipe 86: Sesame Turkey Stir-Fry

Serving Size: 4

Cooking Time: 10 minutes

Ingredients:

- 1/8 tsp. red pepper flakes
- 1 tsp. cornstarch
- 2 tbsp. low-sodium soy sauce
- ½ cup water
- 2 tsp. curry powder
- 1 tbsp. honey
- 2 tsp. sesame oil
- 1 onion, sliced into thin wedges
- 1 sweet red pepper, julienned
- 2 cups cooked turkey breast, shredded
- 1 garlic clove, minced
- 2 cups hot cooked brown rice
- 1 green onion, sliced
- toasted sesame seeds, for garnish
- sliced serrano pepper, for garnish

Directions:

1. Combine the first prepared six ingredients in a small bowl until well combined. Heat the prepared oil in a large skillet over medium-high heat. Stir in the onion and red pepper until crisp-tender.
2. Cook for a further minute after adding the garlic. Add the cornstarch mixture to the pan and stir well. Bring to a very hot boil, then reduce to a low heat and simmer for 2 minutes, or until the sauce has thickened. Heat the turkey until it is fully cooked. Add the green onion and mix well. Serve with a side of rice. Top with sesame seeds and serrano pepper and serve.

Nutritional Value: Calories 269; Fat 4g; Carbohydrates 32g; Protein 25g

Recipe 87: Shrimp with Fresh Parsley

Serving Size: 4

Cooking Time: 10 minutes

Ingredients:

- 2 tablespoons butter
- 1 large garlic clove, minced
- 1/4 teaspoon cayenne pepper
- 2 tablespoons chicken broth
- 5 teaspoons lemon juice
- 1 tablespoon minced fresh parsley
- 1/2 teaspoon salt
- 1-pound uncooked shrimp (26-30 per pound), peeled and deveined

Directions:

1. Place the butter, garlic and cayenne pepper in a 9-inch bowl. microwave-safe cake plate. Cover and microwave until butter is melted, about 1 minute. Add the wine, lemon juice, parsley and salt. Add the shrimp; toss to coat.
2. Cover and heat in microwave until shrimp turn pink, 2-3 minutes. Stir before serving.

Nutritional Value: Calories 190; Fat 7.8g; Carbohydrates 2.3g; Protein 26.2g

Recipe 88: Tender Turkey with Herbs

Serving Size: 6

Cooking Time: 6 hours

Ingredients:

- 88 oz of turkey crown
- salt to taste
- black pepper to taste
- 5 tsp of rosemary
- 5 tsp of thyme
- 1 onion
- 3.9 oz of butter
- 8.8 oz of celery leaves
- 12.7 fl oz of white wine

Directions:

1. Season the turkey crown with black pepper and salt. Place rosemary, thyme sprigs, onion, and butter slices in the cavity of the turkey crown. Combine the celery leaves, remaining onion, and remaining herbs in a slow cooker.
2. Place the prepared turkey crown on top of the veggies and herbs with the top facing down. Cover the white wine on the stove. Cook on high for about 6 hours. Remove the saucepan from the oven and cover with foil. Allow 15 minutes for the turkey breast to rest before slicing.

Nutritional Value: Calories 150; Fat 6g; Carbohydrates 2g; Protein 20g

Recipe 89: Turkey Patties with Dark Onion Gravy

Serving Size: 4

Cooking Time: 20 minutes

Ingredients:

- 1 pound 93% lean ground turkey
- 1 tablespoon flour
- 1 1/3 cups chopped yellow onion
- 1 tablespoon sodium-free chicken bouillon granules

Directions:

1. Shape the prepared turkey into 4 patties, about 1/2 inch thick; sprinkle with 1/8 teaspoon salt and 1/8 teaspoon pepper, if desired.
2. Heat a large skillet over medium-high heat. Add flour and cook 3 minutes or until beginning to lightly brown, stirring constantly. Set aside on separate plate.
3. Coat skillet with cooking spray, add onions, and cook 3 minutes or until beginning to brown on edges. Push to one side of the skillet, add the turkey patties, reduce to medium heat, and cook 6 minutes on each side or until no longer pink in center.
4. Remove the turkey patties from the onion mixture and set aside on serving platter. Add 1 cup water and bouillon granules to the onions, sprinkle with the flour and 1/8 teaspoon salt and 1/8 teaspoon pepper. Stir and cook until thickened, about 1 1/2 to 2 minutes. Spoon over patties.

Nutritional Value: Calories 210; Fat 10g; Carbohydrates 8g; Protein 22g

Recipe 90: Zucchini Carbonara

Serving Size: 4

Cooking Time: 25 minutes

Ingredients:

- 6 slices of bacon, cut into pieces
- 1 red onion, finely chopped
- 3 zucchini, cut into noodles
- 1 cup peas
- ½ teaspoon sea salt
- 3 garlic cloves, minced
- 3 large eggs, beaten
- 1 tablespoon heavy cream
- Pinch red pepper flakes
- ½ cup grated parmesan cheese (optional, for garnish)

Directions:

1. In a large-sized pan, cook the bacon until browned over medium heat, about 5 minutes. Transfer the bacon to a plate.
2. Add the onion to the bacon fat and cook, stirring, until soft, 3 to 5 minutes. Add the zucchini, peas, and salt. Cook, stirring until the zucchini softens, about 3 minutes. Add the garlic in and cook.
3. Whisk the eggs, cream, and red pepper flakes in a small bowl. Add to the vegetables.
4. Remove the pan from the heat and stir for 3 minutes, allowing the pan's heat to cook the eggs without setting them.
5. Return the bacon to the pan and mix well.
6. Serve topped with parmesan cheese, if desired.

Nutritional Value: Calories 327; Fat 24g; Carbohydrates 7g; Protein 14.1g

Chapter 4: Dessert Recipes

Recipe 91: Baked Maple Custard

Serving Size: 6

Cooking Time: 1 hour 15 minutes

Ingredients:

- 2½ cups half-and-half
- ½ cup egg substitute
- 3 cups boiling water
- ¼ cup S1plenda
- 2 tablespoons sugar-free maple syrup
- 2 teaspoons vanilla
- Dash nutmeg
- Non-stick cooking spray

Directions:

1. Heat oven to 325°F.
2. Lightly grease the 6 ramekins with cooking spray.
3. Combine half-n-half, egg yolks, Splenda, vanilla, and nutmeg in a large bowl.
4. Pour evenly into prepared custard cups.
5. Place the cups in a 13x9-inch baking dish.
6. Pour boiling water around the cup, careful not to splash it. Bake the cups for 1 hour and 15 minutes.
7. Remove the cups from the large-sized pan and let them cool completely.
8. Cover and let cool overnight.
9. Drizzle with maple syrup before serving.

Nutritional Value: Calories 190; Fat 12g; Carbohydrates 10g; Protein 5g

Recipe 92: Blueberry Crisp

Serving Size: 10

Cooking Time: 4 hours

Ingredients:

- 1/4 cup butter, melted
- 24 oz. blueberries, frozen
- 3/4 teaspoon salt
- 1 1/2 cups rolled oats, coarsely ground
- 3/4 cup almond flour, blanched
- 1/4 cup coconut oil, melted
- 6 tablespoons sweetener
- 1 cup pecans or walnuts, coarsely chopped

Directions:

1. Using a non-stick cooking spray, spray the slow cooker pot well.
2. Into a bowl, add ground oats and chopped nuts along with salt, blanched almond flour, brown sugar, stevia granulated sweetener, and then stir in the coconut/butter mixture. Stir well to combine.
3. When done, spread crisp topping over blueberries. Cook for 3-4 hours, until the mixture has become bubbling hot and you can smell the blueberries.
4. Serve while still hot with the whipped cream or the ice cream if desired. Enjoy!

Nutritional Value: Calories 261; Fat 16.6g; Carbohydrates 32g; Protein 4g

Recipe 93: Blueberry Muffins

Serving Size: 3

Cooking Time: 1 hour

Ingredients:

- 1/2 cup of Blueberries
- 3/4 cup of Teff Flour
- 3/4 cup of Spelt Flour
- 1/3 cup of Agave Syrup
- 1/2 teaspoon of Pure Sea Salt
- 1 cup of Coconut Milk
- 1/4 cup of Sea Moss Gel (optional, check information)
- Grape Seed Oil

Directions:

1. Preheat your oven to 365 degrees Fahrenheit.
2. Grease or line 6 standard muffin cups.
3. Add Teff, Spelt flour, Pure Sea Salt, Coconut Milk, Sea Moss Gel, and Agave Syrup to a large bowl. Mix them together.
4. Add Blueberries to the mixture and mix well.
5. Divide muffin batter among the 6 muffin cups.
6. Bake for 30 minutes until golden brown.
7. Serve and enjoy your Blueberry Muffins!

Nutritional Value: Calories 165; Fat 0.7g; Carbohydrates 12g; Protein 1.4g

Recipe 94: Carrot Cupcakes

Serving Size: 12

Cooking Time: 35 minutes

Ingredients:

- 2 cup carrots, grated
- 1 cup low fat cream cheese, soft
- 2 eggs
- 1-2 teaspoons skim milk
- ½ cup coconut oil, melted
- ¼ cup coconut flour
- ¼ cup Splenda
- ¼ cup honey
- 2 teaspoon vanilla, divided
- 1 teaspoon baking powder
- 1 teaspoon cinnamon
- Non-stick cooking spray

Directions:

1. Preheat the oven to 350°F.
2. Gently spray the muffin pan or use a paper pan.
3. Combine the flour, baking powder, and cinnamon in a large bowl.
4. Place the carrots, eggs, oil, Splenda, and vanilla in the food processor. Add the dry ingredients and combine well. Mix until the ingredients are combined, but there are still large pieces of carrot remaining.
5. Pour evenly into the prepared pan and fill the cup 2/3 full.
6. Bake for 30-35 minutes until the dough passes the dough. Take out of the oven and let cool.
7. In a small bowl, mix fast until the cream cheese, honey, and vanilla are tender.
8. Add little milk at a time, stirring with each addition, stirring until the frosting is creamy enough to spread quickly.
9. When the cupcakes have cooled, sprinkle about 2 tablespoons of frosting on each.
10. Let excellent until served.

Nutritional Value: Calories 160; Fat 10g; Carbohydrates 13g; Protein 4g

Recipe 95: Chocolate Orange Bread Pudding

Serving Size: 8

Cooking Time: 35 minutes

Ingredients:

- 4 cups french baguette cubes
- 1 ½ cups skim milk
- 3 eggs, lightly beaten
- 1-2 teaspoon orange zest, grated
- ¼ cup Splenda
- ¼ cup sugar-free chocolate ice cream topping
- 3 tablespoon unsweetened cocoa powder
- 1 teaspoon vanilla
- ¾ teaspoon cinnamon

Directions:

1. Heat the oven to 350°F.
2. In a medium bowl, combine the Splenda and cocoa. Whisk milk, egg, zest, vanilla, and cinnamon until well combined.
3. Place square bread on an 8-inch square baking sheet. Pour the milk mixture.
4. Bake pudding for 35 minutes or until a medium knife is clean. Let cool for 5-10 minutes.
5. Plate the cake and sprinkle lightly with an ice cream topping. Serve and enjoy.

Nutritional Value: Calories 139; Fat 2g; Carbohydrates 22g; Protein 6g

Recipe 96: Fig and Walnut Yogurt Tarts

Serving Size: 6

Cooking Time: 20 minutes

Ingredients:

- 1 oz. crumbled goat cheese
- ¼ cup nonfat, plain Greek yogurt
- 2 tbsp. freshly squeezed orange juice
- 12 mini phyllo dough shells
- 12 leaves fresh mint, chopped
- 12 walnut halves
- 4 large fresh figs, chopped

Directions:

1. Combine yogurt, goat cheese and orange juice in a small mixing bowl.
2. Fill 1 tbsp. of the cheese mixture into each phyllo shell.
3. Place a walnut half, 1 mint leaf, and a fig slice on top of each.
4. Keep it refrigerated before serving and enjoy.

Nutritional Value: Calories 130; Fat 7g; Carbohydrates 14g; Protein 4g

Recipe 97: Frozen Lemon and Blueberry

Serving Size: 4

Cooking Time: 10 minutes

Ingredients:

- 6 cup fresh blueberries
- 8 sprigs fresh thyme
- ¾ cup light brown sugar
- 1 teaspoon lemon zest
- ¼ cup lemon juice
- 2 cups water

Directions:

1. Add blueberries, thyme and sugar in a pan over medium heat.
2. Cook for 6 to 8 minutes.
3. Transfer mixture to a blender.
4. Remove thyme sprigs.
5. Stir in the remaining ingredients.
6. Pulse until smooth.
7. Strain mixture and freeze for 1 hour.

Nutritional Value: Calories 178; Fat 5g; Carbohydrates 20g; Protein 3g

Recipe 98: Lemon Chiffon with Fresh Berries

Serving Size: 6

Cooking Time: 1 hour 20 minutes

Ingredients:

- 1/3 cup fresh lemon juice
- 4 large eggs
- 3 cup fresh berries
- ½ cup granulated Splenda

Directions:

1. In a saucepan, combine the Splenda and lemon juice. Heat and whisk until the sugar is completely dissolved. Remove the pan from the heat. In a mixing dish, crack the eggs and whisk them thoroughly. While stirring, slowly add the lemon sugar mixture into the eggs.
2. Return the egg mix to the pot after 1 minute of whisking. Cook for several minutes over low to medium heat, whisking constantly, until the egg mixture thickens. Depending on your equipment, this will take 2-5 minutes.
3. When the mixture coats the back of a spoon, it's time to take it off the heat. Refrigerate for at least one hour. As it cools, it will actually thicken even more. Spoon berries over some of the lemon chiffon in a dessert dish or glass, or stack lemon cream and berries. Garnish with berries.

Nutritional Value: Calories 190; Fat 3g; Carbohydrates 11g; Protein 5g

Recipe 99: Nut Squares

Serving Size: 10

Cooking Time: 10 minutes

Ingredients:

- 2 cups of almonds, pumpkin seeds, sunflower seeds and walnuts
- ½ cup of desiccated coconut
- 1 tablespoon of chia seeds
- ¼ teaspoon of salt
- 2 tablespoons of coconut oil
- 1 teaspoon of vanilla extract
- 3 tablespoons of almond or peanut butter
- 1/3 cup of sukrin gold fiber syrup

Directions:

1. Line a square baking tin with a baking paper; then lightly grease it with cooking spray
2. Chop all the nuts roughly; then slightly grease it too, you can also leave them as whole
3. Mix the nuts in a large bowl; then combine them in a large bowl with the coconut, the chia seeds and the salt
4. In a microwave-proof bowl; add the coconut oil; then add the vanilla, the coconut butter or oil, the almond butter and the fiber syrup and microwave the mixture for about 30 seconds
5. Stir your ingredients together very well; then pour the melted mixture right on top of the nuts
6. Press the prepared mixture into your prepared baking tin with the help of the back of a measuring cup and push very well
7. Freeze your treat for about 1 hour before cutting it
8. Cut your frozen nut batter into small cubes or squares of the same size.

Nutritional Value: Calories 268; Fat 5g; Carbohydrates 14g; Protein 2g

Recipe 100: Peanut Butter Cups

Serving Size: 4

Cooking Time: 10 minutes

Ingredients:

- 1 packet plain gelatin
- ¼ cup sugar substitute
- 2 cups nonfat cream
- ½ teaspoon vanilla
- ¼ cup low-fat peanut butter
- 2 tablespoons unsalted peanuts, chopped

Directions:

1. Mix gelatin, sugar substitute and cream in a pan.
2. Let sit for 5 minutes.
3. Place over medium heat and cook until gelatin has been dissolved.
4. Stir in vanilla and peanut butter.
5. Pour into custard cups. Chill for 3 hours.
6. Top with the peanuts and serve.

Nutritional Value: Calories 171; Fat 13g; Carbohydrates 21g; Protein 6.8g

11. Conclusion

Type 2 diabetes is a condition that's created when glucose levels build up in your bloodstream. It's a common condition that's often triggered by certain lifestyle choices. But the likelihood of a diagnosis can also be increased by genetics, age, and heritage.

Type 2 diabetes can be managed — and even reversed — with certain lifestyle changes. For more severe cases, medication is available.

If you've been diagnosed with type 2 diabetes, talk with your doctor about developing a treatment plan that works for your lifestyle. Because this condition is so common, there's a plethora of resources and first-person accounts to help you on your journey towards managing — or breaking free from — type 2 diabetes.

Whichever diet or eating pattern you choose to follow, it's best to eat a full variety of nutrient-rich foods and practice portion management.

Make an effort to limit your consumption of saturated fats, trans fats, high cholesterol foods, and added sugars.

Your doctor or dietitian can also help you develop a sustainable meal planning approach that fits your health needs and lifestyle

People checking their blood sugar levels with a blood glucose meter will also use a device called a lancet to prick their finger. While the idea of drawing blood might cause distress for some people, lancing the skin to obtain a blood sample should be a gentle, simple procedure. Many meters require only a teardrop-sized sample of blood.

A person may also find the following tips useful:

- Using their fingertips to obtain a blood sample. While some meters allow samples from other test sites, such as the thighs and upper arms, the fingertips or outer palms produce more accurate results.

- Cleaning their skin with soapy, warm water to avoid food residue entering the device and distorting the reading.

- Choosing a small, thin lancet for maximum comfort.

- Adjusting the lancet's depth settings for comfort.

- Taking blood from the side of their finger, as this causes less pain. Using the middle finger, ring finger, and little finger may be more comfortable.

- Teasing blood to the surface in a "milking" motion rather than placing pressure at the lancing site.

- Following local regulations for disposing of sharp objects, including lancets.

- While remembering to self-monitor involves people making lifestyle adjustments, it need not be an uncomfortable process.

12. Index

Almond Quinoa with Cranberries, 9
Apple Spiced Overnight Oats, 10
Artichoke Ratatouille Chicken, 72
Avocado and Goat Cheese Toast, 11
Bagel with Poached Egg, 12
Baked Eggs, 13
Baked Maple Custard, 102
Baked Penne Pasta, 40
Baked Turkey Spaghetti, 73
Banana Bread French Toast, 14
Basil Grilled Shrimp, 74
Beef and Mushroom Casserole, 42
Black Bean and Egg Tacos, 15
Blueberry Crisp, 103
Blueberry Muffins, 104
Brussels Sprout with Fried Eggs, 16
Bulgur Porridge, 17
Butter Beef and Spinach, 43
Buttery Lemon Chicken, 44
Buttery Pot Roast, 45
Cabbage and Meat Gravy, 46
Cajun Coconut Cream Prawns, 75
Carrot Cupcakes, 105
Cauliflower Cups, 18
Cauliflower Fritters, 19
Cheesy Beef and Broccoli, 47
Chicken and Apricot Tagine, 76
Chicken Casablanca, 48
Chicken Fajitas, 77
Chicken Nacho Casserole, 20
Chicken Ricotta, 49
Chicken with Bell Pepper Thyme Sauce, 78
Chili Pork Tenderloin, 79
Chocolate Orange Bread Pudding, 106
Cinnamon Chicken, 80
Crispy Dill Salmon, 50
Crusted Red Snapper, 81
Curry Turkey Stir-Fry, 82
Egg and Ham Burrito, 21
Egg and Spinach Breakfast Burritos, 22
Feta and Sun-Dried Tomatoes Prawns, 51
Feta Scrambled Egg Wraps, 23
Fig and Walnut Yogurt Tarts, 107
Frozen Lemon and Blueberry, 108
Garlic Galore Rotisserie Chicken, 52

Garlic Honey Chicken, 53
Ginger Cod Chard Bake, 83
Halibut Ceviche with Cilantro, 84
Hawaiian Chicken Packets, 54
Herb-Grilled Bass, 85
Honey French Toast, 24
Lamb and Pine Nut Aubergine, 55
Lamb Shanks with Burgundy Sauce, 56
Lemon Chiffon with Fresh Berries, 109
Lemon Pepper Tilapia with Broccoli and Carrots, 57
Lime and Orange Grilled Scallops, 86
Lime Lamb Chops, 58
Lime Pulled Pork, 59
Maple Pork with Figs, 60
Mushroom Breakfast Burrito, 25
Mussels in Tomato Sauce, 87
Nut Squares, 110
Omelet with Turmeric, 27
Orange Tilapia, 88
Parmesan Herb Frittata, 28
Parsley Chicken Breast, 29
Peanut Butter Cups, 111
Peppery Halibut Fillet with Beans, 89
Pistachios and Herb Halibut, 61
Pork Chops with Apple Stuffing, 62
Potato-Bacon Gratin, 30
Pumpkin Pancakes, 31
Quinoa Burrito, 32
Ricotta and Turkey Bell Peppers, 90
Roast Chicken Casserole, 63
Roast Pork Tenderloin with Apple Slaw, 64
Roasted Beef with Shallot Sauce, 91
Roasted Sea Bass, 92
Roasted Tilapia and Tomatoes with Garlic, 93
Rosemary Chicken, 94
Salisbury Steak in Mushroom Sauce, 66
Salmon Fish Cakes, 95
Salmon in Ginger Cream, 96
Sausage Pasta, 67
Sausage Tortilla Breakfast Bake, 33
Savory Egg Muffins, 34
Scrambled Yellow Tofu, 35
Sesame Chicken with Couscous, 68
Sesame Turkey Stir-Fry, 97

Shrimp with Fresh Parsley, 98
Spicy Jalapeno Popper Deviled Eggs, 36
Sweet and Tangy Salmon, 69
Sweet Potato Hash, 37
Tender Turkey with Herbs, 99
Thyme Turkey Breast, 70

Turkey Patties with Dark Onion Gravy, 100
Walnut and Oat Granola, 38
Walnut and Oat-Crusted Cod, 71
Zucchini and Yellow Pepper Scramble, 39
Zucchini Carbonara, 101

Made in the USA
Columbia, SC
12 December 2022